ACTING & STAGE MOVEMENT

For Amateurs & Professionals

Foreword by Sir Donald Wolfit

Part I:

ACTING

by Edwin C. White

Preface by W. J. Mayhead

Part II:

STAGE MOVEMENT

by Marguerite Battye

Preface by Margaret Leighton

MERIWETHER PUBLISHING LTD.
Colorado Springs, Colorado

Meriwether Publishing Ltd., Publisher
P.O. Box 7710
Colorado Springs, CO 80933

Cover design: Michelle Gallardo

The Library of Congress has cataloged the first printing of this title as
follows:

White, Edwin C.
    Acting and stage movement / foreword by Donald Wolfit. 1st ed. —
    Colorado Springs, CO: Meriwether Pub., [1985], c1963.

    181 p., [26] p. of plates: ill., ports.; 20 cm.

    Cover title: Acting & stage movement for amateurs & professionals.
    Reprint. Previously published: New York: Arc Books, 1963.
    Includes indexes.
    Acting / By Edwin C. White; preface by W. J. Mayhead — Stage movement /
    by Marguerite Battye; preface by Margaret Leighton.
    ISBN 0-916260-30-5 (pbk.)

    1. Acting.   2. Movement (Acting)   3. Amateur theater.   I. Battye,
    Marguerite.   II. Title: III. Title: Acting & stage movement for
    amateurs & professionals.

    PN2061.W48   1985   792'.028-dc19   85-60573

    Library of Congress   AACR 2 MARC

5   6   7   8   9   99   98   97

FOREWORD

by Sir Donald Wolfit, C.B.E.

THIS book is intended for those who have come to know the indefinable magic of the theatre. Their first experience of this may have arisen out of regular theatregoing, with memorable performances to give pleasure in recollection, or through personal work done to advance the Amateur Theatre.

This magic invariably stirs in the mind of the theatre-lover the desire for further knowledge of all the activities that contribute to the complex Art of the Theatre— acting, producing, costuming, make-up, lighting.

In schools and factories, in clubs and civic centres, interest that is created in the theatre is often followed by the determination to become a producer or a player, or to work "behind the scenes." But interest is not enough; knowledge is necessary. Some of this is, no doubt, acquired in haphazard fashion. This volume will be of practical assistance to all to whom it is designed to appeal, thus adding knowledge to interest and strengthening what is often the irresistible magnetism of the theatre.

CONTENTS

Part I:
ACTING

PREFACE
(Acting)

by W. J. Mayhead

I HAVE been but an occasional dabbler in the art of acting, and, in the main, my interests have been confined to Shakespeare; the author of this Handbook has travelled widely in the realms of drama and become a recognized authority. His former book was the best of its kind that I had hitherto met, and in this, it seems to me, he betters his best. My long association with him has taught me much and given many happy memory-pictures which enrich the common-room of later life.

Beginners come to realize that much of the fun and joy and value in amateur dramatics derive from playing as a team under the guidance of one to whom "the *play's* the thing" and that the smallest part, well played, is essential to the success of the whole.

Many years ago I was playing Gratiano to the author's Shylock. I had "made-up," as I thought, adequately —didn't want to overdo it—but at the end of the first scene, he said "Put more colour on your face, you look ghastly!" I have used this memory many times in warning students against the danger of under-acting *and* under-speaking, a danger not confined to amateurs. Recently, at one of the chief London theatres, the speech of some of the players was such that only a sense of propriety prevented my calling out, "'Stay, you imperfect speakers,' and put more colour in your voice."

In his lecturette to the Players, Hamlet surely gave the

last word on the subject of "ham" acting versus so-
called "naturalism." The powers forbid that we should
return to the days when the actor "strutted and bel-
lowed," "for anything so overdone is from the purpose
of playing," but he must "be not too tame neither . . .
or come tardy off."

Reactions often produce evils as great as those against
which they react, and I am inclined to think that this
has happened in production. Largely owing to the—
in his own time—unrewarded pioneer work of William
Poel, the days are gone when the production of a
Shakespearian play often meant a series of elaborate
scenic pictures with *some* of the author's text. But it
seems to me that in recent years, another and more
insidious danger has crept in, with the introduction of
unnecessary and meaningless "business," rushing about
the stage, and movement more suited to ballet. This,
surely, is to place a sort of "iron-curtain" between the
author and the audience.

My mind goes back to Mr. White's own production
of *King Lear*, which is still spoken of, after nearly twenty
years. How it surprised and delighted Ben Greet!

Earnest students of this Handbook will come to
realize what faithful acting demands, and from the
concentrated experience of the author's many years as
actor, producer, and lecturer, the ways in which those
demands may be met. Let them not be discouraged if
they feel that their aim exceeds their grasp, for this
"divine discontent" is the mark of the true artist, and
"the best in this kind are but shadows."

INTRODUCTION
(ACTING)

IT has often been said that *acting cannot be taught*: that an actor is born, not made.

There is truth in this statement, but also exaggeration and much that is misleading. Few actors would deny that they have learnt much from academies of drama and speech, or from experience gained under leading actors and producers. Forbes Robertson frequently expressed his debt to his master, Samuel Phelps, and many actors and actresses have acknowledged with gratitude the advice received from Bernard Shaw. It is true that all great artists possess a quality that is inherent, but no artist can display that quality unless he is master of both his material and his tools.

The purpose of this book is to suggest a method of studying the material of drama and the tools of speech and movement. Its aim is to assist those who wish to act and to interest those who would like to know more about the drama and the theatre. Throughout, the amateur and the student have been kept in mind, but it should be clear that the principles underlying the art of acting are the same for amateur and professional alike.

The study of speech and movement is planned to assist the amateur actor in his task of interpreting character. Emphasis is placed on these two aspects of the actor's art, and on ways in which the actor may gain skill in the use of these indispensable tools. Emphasis is also placed on reading aloud, because the language of drama is speech, not pure literature. It is something that must be spoken and heard; its effects are gained by sound as well as by sense; by the time and speed of speech as well as by the words themselves.

In choosing passages to illustrate ideas or to discuss methods, I have kept in mind plays that are generally well known or easy to obtain. It is hoped that the detailed analysis of some of these passages will suggest methods than can be applied to other plays and characters.

My purpose has been to focus thought and attention upon the essential needs of the actor in the hope that by so doing the principles of interpretation may be learnt.

Acting is an alluring pastime in which joy increases as skill is acquired. But skill can be gained only by patience and perseverance, by knowing the way and pursuing it. It is my hope that what I have written will indicate the way for those wishing to prepare themselves for the actor's task.

Finally, I must express my indebtedness and gratitude to my good friend John Luscombe for his many suggestions, and especially to Mr. Harold Downs for his sound and expert advice and help. My thanks are also due to my very old friend and colleague, Billy Mayhead, for his charming Preface.

CHAPTER I

THE ACTOR'S DILEMMA:
NEED FOR A TECHNIQUE

A PLAY, which is the actor's material, is the story of a selected group of characters, their relationships and intimacies, their conversations and deeds. It is a story that may be read in privacy or in public; but its primary purpose is for presentation to an audience. Indeed it is often stated that a play does not come into being until it is performed upon a stage in a theatre.

In the theatre, or wherever a play, on an ambitious or a modest scale, is performed, an audience witnesses all that is unfolded and becomes a silent participant in all that takes place. In one sense the audience becomes a part of the play, an essential part, for, without its sympathetic participation, that which the author has selected for life will not live. It will be still-born.

Herein lies a dilemma for the actor, either professional or amateur. While he is on intimate terms with other characters in the play, it is, at the same time, necessary for him to communicate all that he says, and does, and thinks, to the audience. There must be complete understanding between the actor and the audience, which must be made to enter into the innermost thoughts and motives of the characters on the stage. The actor must communicate his whole being: his emotions, his desires, his purpose, his background, his thoughts, his words and deeds. The audience must be made to know him more intimately than do any of his intimates on the stage. Thus while the character lives within a world created by the author, the actor's task is to make him live even more completely for the world outside and beyond that of the play itself.

This dilemma imposes upon the actor the need for a technique, or way of acting, so that, on the one hand, he remains within the circle of selected characters, while, on the other hand, he is always in touch with an audience that is outside the orbit of the action.

Technique, then, is as essential for the actor as it is for any other artist. Mere virtuosity or reliance upon chance tricks will not suffice. All artists and craftsmen must know how to achieve their desired purpose, must be able to perform essential tasks, and cultivate skill in the selection of material and method. In all crafts there are skills which all craftsmen must possess. At the same time, however, there is a technique that is personal to the individual craftsman.

Consider for a moment the behaviour of three people in a room. They will behave naturally. They will converse, knit, or read, or even sleep; they will sit, stand, or move; be mobile or static; they will just please themselves. This naturalism, however, may be most undesirable and unsuitable for actors representing these people before an audience in a theatre. Here mere behaviour is not enough, for in the theatre the actor must communicate his thoughts, his actions, and his feelings to the audience. To achieve this he must find a special way, he must impose a technique.

This may be commonplace, but we still see players on the stage hiding each other, or a stage so darkened that we cannot see what is going on, or actors speaking so quietly that it is difficult to hear what they are saying. Criticism of these things is countered by the retort that darkness is the condition of the scene, and that the characters should be holding a confidential conversation. The truth is we may not bring the natural behaviour of either the elements or people on to the stage. The whisper of real life must become the "stage whisper." The theatre is a place for illusion, not realism. The reality of a storm would destroy illusion; the naturalism of human behaviour could be indecorous, even indecent, when witnessed by an audience. Othello kills Desdemona: the actor may not do so; Ophelia loses her wits: if the actress does, she will not be able to simulate her part.

Always the actor must seek a way to create the illusion of reality and truth. He must appear to be natural within the limits imposed by the conditions of the theatre. He must be the Othello of Shakespeare's creation, and the Othello who with Desdemona lives to play another day. Sir Toby Belch and Sir Andrew Aguecheek get very drunk, but there is no reason why either or both should not be interpreted by teetotallers. *Acting is the art of interpretation, not imitation.* It is the task of the actor to find a way of interpretation that will be understood and appreciated by an audience.

Consider a particular stage problem. How will an actor play, in turn, each of the characters Shylock, Bassanio, and Antonio in Act 1, Scene 3, of *The Merchant of Venice*, or in a modern play, the characters of Professor Higgins, Colonel Pickering, and the Dustman Doolittle in Act 2 of *Pygmalion*?

First look at the scene from *The Merchant of Venice*. Shakespeare has provided language for each character.

Tufts Arena Theatre, Tuft College, Medford, Mass., was the scene of G. B. Shaw's "Pygmalion."

Courtesy ANTA

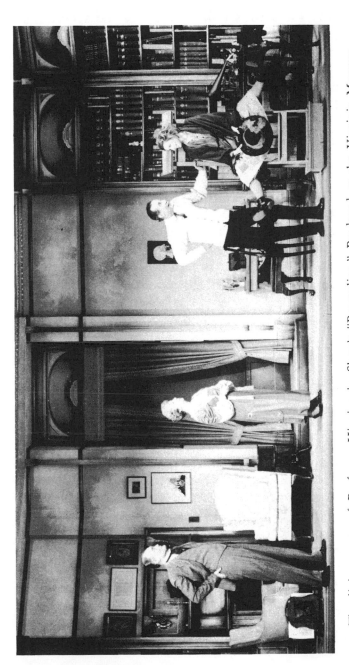

The living room of Professor Higgins in Shaw's "Pygmalion." Produced at the Virginia Museum Theatre, Richmond, Va., February 1962.

Courtesy ANTA

Obviously the actor's task is to study the speeches set
down for each to speak. The characters are not
described as a novelist would describe them. All that
can be known about them must be discovered from the
dialogue. From this one scene all the knowledge
needed for complete interpretation cannot be gained;
it will be necessary to read the whole play carefully
before setting out with certainty. When this has been
done it will be realized that each character possesses a
distinct personality; speaks differently, because each
thinks differently; moves and stands differently. Costume and make-up help to establish identity, but much
more is needed if the audience is to know each as a
human being with an individual creed, separate ambitions, and distinctive mentality. A way must be
found to reveal the eager vitality of Bassanio, his gay
irresponsible nature, his charm, and his affection for
Antonio and distrust of Shylock. To show the sad
Antonio, his aloofness and his steadfastness of character
that has endeared him to all but Shylock, a different
technique must be found. And again a different technique will be needed to interpret the complex character
of Shylock.

First we find *what* we are to show; then *how* we are to
achieve it.

In the first scene of *Pygmalion*, Professor Higgins out-
lines the various stages in the life of Colonel Pickering
from observing him and hearing him talk. *Speech and
bearing reveal the man.* His public school, university,
and army background are reflected in his speech and
deportment, just as is the manner of Doolittle's life.

We discover early in the play that the Professor is
meticulously careful in his studies and his manner of

thinking; that his taste in literature and art is fastidious; but as we read on we find that he is frequently careless about his physical habits; that he fidgets and keeps his hands in his pockets. His enthusiasm, the result of mental excitement, is displayed in physical unrest and action that disturbs others. He is a learned professor whose behaviour is eccentric. His specialized study of phonetics gives him complete command of speech. Normally his own speech is perfect, but he can, and does, imitate the peculiarities of others. His hearing is acute, and his thoughts readily respond to sound and cause audible ejaculations that are sometimes distressing to others.

Comparison of these three characters reveals that a special technique is required for the interpretation of each. Their individual qualities of speech, deportment, and movement demand a distinctive manner of treatment, if their mental and physical qualities are to be appreciated by the audience.

In *Waters of the Moon*, produced at The Theatre Royal, Haymarket, three outstanding actresses, Dame Edith Evans, Dame Sybil Thorndike, and Miss Wendy Hiller gave performances of unique merit. Each presented a character that was individually significant in its mental and physical qualities. Each revealed character by brilliantly weaving movement, repose, and speech into a harmonious whole. The visual memory of each is as distinctive as the auditory. Speech and movement were related and in sympathy with character.

Now read and study the duets between Queen Elizabeth and Mary Fitton in Act 2, Scene 1, and again in Act 4, of Clemence Dane's *Will Shakespeare*. Compare the two ladies. Think of their physical as well as their mental qualities. Think about their relative stations in society; their individual manners and ambitions. Think of their relationship to others as well as to each other. By careful study and by the use of imagination a separate picture of each will be obtained. Queen Elizabeth is unique amongst women. Her position gives her certain advantages, but it is her unique character that enables her to maintain that position. It is for the actress to find those qualities as they are set down in the play, and then by speech and movement to bring them before an audience.

Study first, then find a technique for interpretation.

Technique depends upon power of vocalization and ability to move. Control of both speech and body conveys the picture of the character as it is seen in your mind. The studies of the actor are first the material, which is in the play, and then speech and movement by which he will interpret.

Speaking and doing are the ingredients of acting. What is spoken and done must be found from the play itself. "What shall I do?" is a common appeal at rehearsal. The answer is always in the play. An actor may have to stand still and to listen; then he will have to find a way of doing just that. "I don't know what to do with my hands," or "May I smoke a cigarette, it will give me something to do?" Players are conscious of the need to do something, but often there is not keen awareness that what is done is important. All that is done on the stage is important because it is seen by the audience. A cigarette produced at the wrong moment, a smile, or exaggerated glumness, may detract attention from an essential detail or character. A careless glance or even the slightest movement of head or hand may ruin a scene. A player is part of a scene and is not on the stage just to display talent or to draw attention to his own character. Often his sole purpose is to focus attention upon others. In scenes where several characters are on the stage this is obvious. It was markedly so in *Waters of the Moon*. One outstanding feature of this production was the manner in which the focus of interest moved from one character to another, and how all concerned saw to it that nothing drew attention from the vital character of the moment.

Discipline and control are necessary attributes of the actor's craft.

The art of acting demands both self-discipline and self-criticism. It calls for both critical and imaginative faculties. The actor's field of study is wide. To play Caesar, he should know something of the Romans; to play Higgins, something of phonetics. He should be an observer of men in the world of his own time, and he should acquire a knowledge of the manners, thoughts, and speech of men in other ages. He should have more than a superficial acquaintance with the history and development of drama and the theatre.

Fashions and modes of dramatic expression alter. Great changes have taken place within the theatre itself since Shakespeare's time when plays were performed on an open stage. A revolution since Ibsen wrote has brought into existence both new types of play and fresh techniques of acting.

These changes, however, should not mislead players into thinking that their task is any different from what it was in the past. New ways may have to be found, but the source of what is to be played is still the play, and the actor himself is still the instrument. Voice and body must be exercised to do the actor's bidding. He must be able to relax, and be alert and ready to respond to any stimulus from the play and other players. Care and practice can develop the player's instrument into a thing of beauty, grace, and power. Its possibilities are limited only by individual capacity and will to achieve. Did not Professor Higgins create a Duchess from Liza Doolittle?

The possession of a beautiful instrument is, however, no guarantee that beautiful music will be produced. The player, himself, must cultivate qualities of mind, perception, and perseverance, if he is to interpret the range and depth of human emotions and conflicts found within the plays.

There is a tendency to believe that modern plays must be easier to perform than Shakespeare's plays because the characters are more like those met from day to day. Is this really true? Are we really familiar with such people as those in Somerset Maugham's *The Circle*, Lonsdale's *The Last of Mrs. Cheyney*, or J. B. Priestley's *Laburnum Grove*? Even if we are, it does not follow that actors and actresses can more easily give them life in the theatre. Laurence Irving was far more successful in bringing to life on the stage a Japanese doctor than he was a university professor, although he had held the position of a professor in a French academy.

Characters in a modern play, in any play, are created in the mind of the dramatist, move in a world of his choice, and are limited by his will.

It is often said: "You don't hear people making long speeches as do some of Shakespeare's characters. I want something more natural, dialogue more like that I am used to." In the next chapter I have much to say about speech patterns of everyday life. Here I suggest that the dialogue of the modern play is not always as natural as it seems to be. Noel Coward may be right when he claims that he gives photographic pictures of the morals of our times, but he surely cannot expect us to believe that the speech in *The Vortex* or *Hay Fever* is a dictaphone recording of human dialogue either of this or any other age. This quick-fire chatter, crisp, pert, and sometimes impertinent, is as artificially created as any in our dramatic literature. It is speech selected, polished, and refined, to suit the themes; disciplined and controlled, economic, amusing, and provocative. It is a veneer, brilliantly marked, imposed upon characters of little worth and less morality, revealing the shallow pretentiousness of a self-satisfied and complacent society. It is brilliantly amusing and exciting, art at its most efficient, but neither the characters nor the dialogue is to be met with in daily life.

All dramatic dialogue is speech selected for specific purposes. Speeches in *Pygmalion*, *St. Joan*, and *The Apple Cart* are as long as any in Shakespeare. It would be impossible for the ideas in these plays to be expressed by any other convention. Language fits the ideas and the characters because it is their clothing.

The actor must penetrate the world created by the dramatist and then, in terms of speech and movement, interpret the characters, as seen in his mind, to the audience.

CHAPTER II

"SPEAK THE SPEECH, I PRAY YOU"

"SPEAK the speech, I pray you, as I pronounced it to you, trippingly on the tongue."

Hamlet's advice is not ambiguous. He knew how he wanted the actor to speak and the manner was not left to chance. It was to be related to the matter to be spoken, and delivered in the manner indicated.

There is nothing in this excellent advice to the Players which suggests that the actor's speech should be "natural." On the contrary, it is urged that speech shall be studied and fitting. "Suit the words to the action, the action to the words."

Many who take part in plays give little thought to speech. They just learn words and speak them to the best of their "natural" ability. Everybody possesses natural ability to speak and to act. Herein lies the difference between those who wish to act and those who wish to play an instrument. Any one who is not dumb and who is able to walk can accept a part in a play. Indeed, many do get by with minimum qualifications.

There are those who possess a natural gift for speech, but even the most gifted ultimately fail in the task of interpretation when that which is to be interpreted lies beyond the scope of intuition. The bare truth is that there are really few who possess a natural gift for dramatic speech.

One strange fact about speech is that while a person

readily and unconsciously speaks the normal patterns that are used in everyday life, he does not necessarily recognize these speech patterns when they are set down on the printed page. Ask the average ordinary person to read a simple poem and at once something strange and artificial is heard. He is usually entirely unaware that what he has been asked to read is really simple straightforward language similar to that he himself uses in his daily life.

Our natural speech is something that we have picked up by unconscious imitation. We have imitated patterns but not consciously recognized them as such. When these patterns are set down they appear as a succession of words, not as a speech pattern. Unfortunately, we tend to read the separate words and the reading destroys the pattern of sound.

Hearing Accurately

Sound and speech concern the actor most intimately. He must train himself to hear accurately. But hearing is no easier than observing. Rarely does the faculty just happen. A good observer is a trained observer. Hearing with accuracy can be developed only by careful and conscious effort. The parts played by the consonants and vowels in our language must be consciously observed and heard.

In an age when men read less and listened more it was found that when we pronounced the letter "l" the tongue vibrated with a slow and uncertain trembling, sometimes resembling the motion of water when blown upon. Speak and listen to these lines:

> "Double, double toil and trouble,
> Fire, burn ; and, cauldron, bubble."

As we listen we can almost hear the bubbling of the cauldron.   Listen again to the same consonant in:

> "O what can ail thee, knight-at-arms,
> Alone and palely loitering?"

Notice how perfectly the repetition of the "l"-sound directs attention towards the figure of the Knight and reflects his uncertain and hesitating mood.

Listen to the fun Shakespeare has with the consonants in *A Midsummer Night's Dream*:

> "Whereat with blade, with bloody blameful blade
> He bravely broach'd his boiling bloody breast;
> And Thisby, tarrying in mulberry shade,
> His dagger drew and died."

The humour of alliteration in this scene is irresistible; but equally effective, albeit not humorous, are the consonants in such passages as this from *Romeo and Juliet*:

> "Gallop apace, you fiery-footed steeds,
> Towards Phoebus' lodging: such a waggoner
> As Phaeton would whip you to the west,
> And bring in cloudy night immediately."

The appropriateness of the arresting consonants in the first line is remarkable.   They reflect exactly the frustration in Juliet's mind.   The words themselves might suggest speed, but the consonants linger and struggle, just as thought lingers and struggles in the impatient mind of Juliet awaiting the return of her Romeo.

And what a magical sound is "w" repeated so effectively in "waggoner," "whip," and "west."   A lovely sound this "w," introducing one of the most delightful words in our language—wooing.

Articulation

Precise articulation is necessary not merely for the sake of audibility, but also for expressing the magical and dramatic qualities of sound which, in turn, carries us into the heart of poetry and drama.

I do not apologize for using poetry as examples, for, as Matthew Arnold said: "Poetry is nothing less than the most perfect speech of man." Poets know this to be true, but do the majority of people think of poetry in this way? I hardly think so. A more common opinion is that poetry is something specialized and artificial, remote from life, and sometimes precious. Most people do not hear or read verse as natural speech patterns; they regard verse as a licensed art, which may or may not give them pleasure. They have heard of rhythm, but they think of it as the grammarians do, in terms of iambics, couplets, blank verse, and the like. Few hear rhythm as speech patterns, or even think of verse as a conscious recording of speech, of the ordinary everyday speech of the common man. Indeed, owing to the artificial way in which so many read, the patterns of speech that are readily accepted in the course of living will be regarded as artificial or unusual when read from the printed page.

There is nothing artificial or unusual about the opening line of *The Listeners*. It is just a simple question:

" 'Is there anybody there?' said the Traveller."

How simple and natural too is the opening speech pattern of *Tarantella*:

"Do you remember an Inn, Miranda?
Do you remember an Inn?"

Equally so is the grand and various verse of Shakespeare
a direct recording of speech:

"Let me not to the marriage of true minds
Admit impediments; love is not love
Which alters when it alteration finds,
Or bends with the remover to remove."

"Speak the speech, I pray you" as it is set down.
Speak it easily and straightforwardly and with conviction.   Speak it aloud, become accustomed to its sound,
take delight in the music of the English language.
Unfortunately, there are many like Jessica in *The Merchant of Venice* who are never merry when they hear
sweet music.   To all such I would recall Lorenzo's
reply:

"The man that hath no music in himself,
Nor is not mov'd with concord of sweet sounds,
Is fit for treasons, stratagems, and spoils;
The motions of his spirit are dull as night,
And his affections dark as Erebus:
Let no such man be trusted."

English is the most musical language in the world.   No
other language possesses such variety of vowel sounds.
The abundance of our great lyrical poetry testifies to
this musical quality and gives to us a rich inheritance of
"concord of sweet sounds."

Reading aloud

Reading aloud, especially the great lyrical verse,
familiarizes the reader with the speech patterns of our

language. Make a habit of recognizing these and of speaking them. Often we are tempted to deny that what we find in a poem is a recording of a speech pattern because we have never heard it, or think we have never heard it. We forget that the poet is far more sensitive to sound than we are. I was reminded of this a few years ago when I was staying in a hotel in Devon. It was a chilly August evening and several of the guests were sitting round a fire in the lounge talking. Suddenly an amazing bit of conversation stirred my pulse. Imagine the group—a young girl and a youth on a settee, several older folk in front of the fire, and two or three on the other side. In reply to a question, the youth answered: "Are there any?" "Any?" echoed a young lady, and immediately the girl on the settee said: "No, there is none."

Put the pieces together and we have:

"Are there any, any, no there is none."

You will remember this is a line direct from *The Leaden Echo* by Gerard Manley Hopkins, written about the middle of the nineteenth century.

Such a speech pattern, of course, is more suitable for choral speaking, for it is a pattern recording of more than one voice: a speech pattern which records the interlacing of the thoughts of several people. We find it in the drama of T. S. Eliot: the choruses in *A Murder in a Cathedral* are outstanding examples.

The poet and the dramatist record patterns of sound they have heard. The speaker of verse and the actor must appreciate these patterns and by speaking them make them live in the minds of the audience. Thus reading aloud, both verse forms and dramatic dialogue, becomes an essential exercise for all who wish to act. The actor should both cultivate the habit of listening to speech and acquire the skill of speaking. He should learn patterns of speech. There is a close relation between thought and speech pattern. Learning in this way will compel the actor to think the thoughts that have given rise to the expression of them.

Speech Patterns

The repetition of speech patterns gives to verse that magical quality we call rhythm. All people respond to this quality of language. Even the most unresponsive are sensitive to doggerel and jingle. By persistent reading aloud and listening to others we may develop sensitiveness to other forms of rhythm, from the simplest and most obvious to the majestic declamation of Milton and the splendour and vigour of Shakespeare. Shakespeare was poet as well as dramatist. His verse is the finest recording of speech rhythms in our language. In *A Midsummer Night's Dream* there are eleven various rhythms, all with their own special quality and delight. Read aloud the opening speech of *Twelfth Night*:

"If music be the food of love, play on;
Give me excess of it, that, surfeiting,
The appetite may sicken, and so die."

Read aloud the whole speech. Read it simply, and direct it to an imaginary group of musicians. Keep throughout the simple pattern of speech that is set by the opening line. Master this pattern so that the speech flows easily and "trippingly" on the tongue. Think about the speech as it is spoken and there will be awareness that the musicians respond and that a familiar tune is heard. This will involve a pause before: "That strain again" is spoken. Later it will be appreciated that speech is no longer addressed to the musicians, but is a soliloquy addressed to the speaker and indirectly to the audience.

Read aloud Portia's speech in Act 4, Scene 1, of *The Merchant of Venice* beginning:

"The quality of mercy is not strain'd."

Think of each separate idea and the speech pattern as you read; think of the actual person being addressed. Remember this is not a speech that has to be learnt and recited. It is something spoken to an individual who is threatening to harm, perhaps kill, a being you have every wish to save. It is an expression of thought and idea, spontaneously aroused by Shylock's bitter obstinacy against all pleas for mercy. The thoughts and their expression may not be as slow in the theatre as they used to be, and, indeed, still frequently are, in the cinema. Nevertheless, the audience will respond to the reality and truth of this scene only if the actress translates accurately the patterns of thought and speech.

Read aloud Viola's speech in Act 1, Scene 5, of *Twelfth Night* beginning:

"Make me a willow cabin at your gate"

and also Viola's reply to Duke Orsino in Act 2, Scene 4, of the same play beginning:

"A blank, my lord.   She never told her love."

The pattern of speech in each of these passages is simple and direct.   Each statement clothes a thought or picture, and as thoughts accumulate and pile up on one another

Changling Simpleton

S^r I Falstafe Hostes Clause

THE RED BULL PLAYHOUSE, CLERKENWELL
Shakespeare's plays were for some time acted at this theatre

we listen to most moving revelations of the mind and emotions of Viola. Here are both poetry and drama.

In very different mood moves Gratiano's speech in the first scene of *The Merchant of Venice*:

"Let me play the fool:
With mirth and laughter let old wrinkles come;
And let my liver rather heat with wine
Than my heart cool with mortifying groans.
Why should a man, whose blood is warm within,
Sit like his grandsire cut in alabaster?
Sleep when he wakes, and creep into the jaundice
By being peevish? I tell thee what, Antonio,—
I love thee, and it is my love that speaks,—
There are a sort of men, whose visages
Do cream and mantle like a standing pond;
And do a wilful stillness entertain,
With purpose to be drest in an opinion
Of wisdom, gravity, profound conceit:
As who should say, 'I am Sir Oracle,
And when I ope my lips, let no dog bark!'
O my Antonio, I do know of these,
That therefore only are reputed wise
For saying nothing; when I am very sure,
If they should speak, would almost damn those ears,
Which hearing them, would call their brothers fools.
I'll tell thee more of this another time;
But fish not, with this melancholy bait,
For this fool-gudgeon, this opinion."

Read it aloud and think upon its changing moods. Try to catch not only the speech patterns but the varying speeds at which these patterns move. There are fun and gaiety, followed by a sudden expression of sincere

Raymond Massey is shown here as Brutus in the American Shakespeare Festival Theatre's production of "Julius Caesar."

Courtesy ANTA

The Court Scene, "The Merchant of Venice," by Shakespeare, in a production by the Dartmouth Players.

Courtesy ANTA

affection, which shyly intrudes and gives place to what is almost bombastic declamation and exaggeration. The speech is a wonderful combination of music and sense, of frivolity and serious purpose, of lighthearted fun and friendliness. Direct speech is wedded to the tune and melody of the poet.

The first movement is in two sections each demanding slightly different emphasis and speed. The first section is light and gay. The question beginning: "Why should a man" puts a brake on the pace, while a slightly greater emphasis will stress the rhetorical nature of the question. The second movement comes abruptly and confidentially. It is quiet and sincere; but it seems that Gratiano's nature is at war with his desire to express his more deeply felt thoughts, and gradually the third movement imposes itself with dogmatic declamation. The sincere mood gives way to exaggerated expression and humorous philosophy, which is later described by Bassanio as "an infinite deal of nothing."

It is not an easy speech. For one thing it is fairly long, and to sustain interest and to reveal its purpose care will need to be taken to time accurately the changes of mood and intention. Timing and phrasing are of the utmost importance. They mark the true artist in speech, just as they do in singing. By timing, the artist assures the correct impact of words and thoughts; by phrasing, he points the right emphasis of ideas.

The speeches of Enobarbus in Act 2, Scene 2, of *Antony and Cleopatra* present a picture of rare beauty, painted with words of "colour, bloom, and aroma." Description is direct, straightforward, and simple. It results from accurate and objective observation, given by one who loathes the subject he describes. It is a

soldier's estimate of the power of an enemy, neither
exaggerating nor under-estimating that power. It is
at once a picture of Cleopatra and a revelation of her
power to ruin his beloved master.

Read aloud and learn:

"The barge she sat in, like a burnish'd throne,
   Burn'd on the water: the poop was beaten gold;
   Purple the sails, and so perfumèd, that
   The winds were love-sick with them; the oars were
      silver,
   Which to the tune of flutes kept stroke, and made
   The water, which they beat, to follow faster,
   As amorous of their strokes. For her own person,
   It beggar'd all description: she did lie
   In her pavilion—cloth-of-gold of tissue—
   O'er picturing that Venus where we see
   The fancy outwork nature: on each side her
   Stood pretty dimpled boys, like smiling Cupids,
   With divers-coloured fans, whose wind did seem
   To glow the delicate cheeks which they did cool,
   And what they undid, did."

"Her gentlewomen, like the Nereides,
   So many mermaids, tended her i' the eyes,
   And made their bends adornings: at the helm
   A seeming mermaid steers; the silken tackle
   Swell with the touches of those flower-soft hands,
   That yarely frame the office. From the barge
   A strange invisible perfume hits the sense
   Of the adjacent wharfs. The city cast
   Her people out upon her; and Antony,
   Enthron'd i' the market place, did sit alone,
   Whistling to the air; which, but for vacancy,

Had gone to gaze on Cleopatra too,
And made a gap in nature."

"Age cannot wither her, nor custom stale
Her infinite variety; other women cloy
The appetites they feed; but she makes hungry
Where most she satisfies; for vilest things
Become themselves in her; that the holy priests
Bless her when she is riggish."

Read it aloud straightforwardly, but with conscious awareness of all the details it describes. Think upon the scene, the objects described and, as far as possible, the thoughts of Enobarbus as he contemplates this evil influence. Notice the alliteration and how the consonants delay speech, and help to concentrate thought on the picture of the royal barge upon the water. Appropriate articulation of consonants is essential, for they possess dramatic qualities. Give appropriate articulation to the two "p's" in the word "poop," and full enunciation to the diphthong "oo." It is a long word for so few letters. Notice how long it takes to say "perfumèd." Linger on these words and there will be realization of the disgust Enobarbus feels, even though he reports truth, which, in its total effect, is one of great and undeniable beauty.

Isolated from its text and character this is one of the most beautiful passages in our language; within the scene, spoken by Enobarbus, it is one of the most dramatic and purposeful speeches to be found anywhere. It displays a picture of great wealth and colour; a picture of wanton waste of precious material, almost as wanton as the central figure herself. It also displays the pathetic figure of the great Antony, master of the world, sitting alone in the market place.   In Enobarbus's mind Antony should be the central figure, he should be the one the mob should come to applaud.   For Enobarbus the world is insane, its people have lost all sense of what is right and fit.   Antony and Rome are his world, and he expects both to receive the respect and adulation due to them.   He cannot fully grasp the situation that is forced upon him.   He sees and describes what is really incredible, so incredible that he is astonished that Nature herself has not denied her own inevitable laws.

Direct and Straightforward Speech

Speak the speech as Shakespeare has pronounced it. Do not, as so many do, try to improve it by overlaying it with your own emotion and your own appreciation of the beauty of language.   Speak it with due regard to articulation of consonants, enunciation of vowels, appropriate length and emphasis of words, and the intensity of thoughts.   Speak easily and comfortably. The description is direct and simple; keep speech direct and straightforward.   The thoughts are clear and definite.   Do not worry about variety; there is suffi-cient variety in the language itself.   There is variety of description, of speed, of consonants and of vowels, of colour and mood.   There are beauty, pathos, and character.

Sometimes speech is fraught with passion, and the speaker may rightly let himself go.   The vigour and intensity of speech bear a relationship to the particular character and the emotion felt and expressed.

Examine the speech of Marullus in the first scene of *Julius Caesar*:

"Wherefore rejoice? What conquest brings he home?
What tributaries follow him to Rome,
To grace in captive bonds his chariot wheels?
You blocks, you stones, you worse than senseless
    things!
O you hard hearts, you cruel men of Rome,
Knew you not Pompey?   Many a time and oft
Have you climb'd up to walls and battlements,
To towers and windows, yea, to chimney tops,
Your infants in your arms, and there have sat
The live-long day, with patient expectation,
To see great Pompey pass the streets of Rome.
And when you saw his chariot but appear,
Have you not made an universal shout,
That Tiber trembled underneath her banks,
To hear the replication of your sounds
Made in her concave shores?
And do you now put on your best attire?
And do you now cull out a holiday?
And do you now strew flowers in his way
That comes in triumph over Pompey's blood?
Be gone!
Run to your houses, fall upon your knees,
Pray to the gods to intermit the plague
That needs must light on this ingratitude."

Try to get a mental picture of Marullus. He is a
Tribune of Rome. Think upon his normal relationship with the plebeian, his contempt for their way of
living and their manner of thought. Think upon his
natural bearing and his sense of authority. Visualize
him against the social background of his time. All these
things have their influence on his normal way of

speaking and his attitude to a plebeian mob. He sees himself as a being far removed from the ordinary citizen. He is not of their element. He possesses dignity and authority, he is assured of himself and demands respect as a right. In any circumstances he will speak with forthright conviction expecting what he says to carry the weight of authority.

The circumstances in which we find him are, however, not those of the ordinary, everyday Rome. Caesar is returning triumphant, and the crowd is out to welcome and cheer him. Marullus was an adherent of Pompey and he distrusts Caesar. His passion is at once political and personal. His anger is intellectual as well as emotional, it is contemptuous and vigorous. He attempts neither to argue nor justify, he hurls authority at the mob with the assurance that they will give way to his imperious commands. He whips the plebeians with a torrent of abuse which allows no response save that of obedience. Compare the speech of Flavius which follows, and at once it will be realized that this good friend senses the need to restore some degree of moderation into the scene.

Read the speech aloud and notice that the rhythm is one of thought and ideas. The impetus of speech comes directly from the thoughts. Passion rises with each fresh outburst. Rhetorical questions give place to scornful sneers, which are followed in turn by further rhetoric and the command "Be gone!" which is given the time length of a whole line of verse.

Read again and again, until each fresh idea is expressed as a direct result of thought. The speech does not move smoothly; it is often staccato, rising to a crescendo of volume which reduces the mob to immobility. The first "Wherefore rejoice?" silences the too-familiar crowd, while the more rational questions which follow compel attention, and reveal the first hint of the political situation in which the play moves. Then the whip is unloosed, each lash cuts deeper into the flesh. Speech is incisive and bitter. Notice how the repeated "s"-sound hisses and snarls.

It is not beauty of sound or colour which claims attention here. It is the passion of rhetoric and the dramatic clash between the individual and the crowd. Speech reveals character and passion. It sets before us the haughty Tribune against the background of the common people, and it reveals him angry and contemptuous. At the same time, we are made aware that it is not the crowd alone that is responsible for this outburst. The deeper cause lies in the defeat of Pompey and the triumph of Caesar; the mental disturbance of Marullus is a result of civil war. This is the prelude to the disturbance which is to overthrow Caesar. It is pure drama.

Very different is the passion of Shylock in Act 3, Scene 1, of *The Merchant of Venice*. Here is a mind racked and tortured by many conflicting thoughts and emotions. The language reveals a soul tormented by the rebellion of his dearly loved daughter, her disloyalty to both him and their creed; a mind overwhelmed by the loss of wealth and jewels, prized for their worth and their sentimental value; a being tossed hither and thither from a great sense of wrong to an even greater desire for revenge. Self-pity and self-assertion struggle for mastery. He is like a ship being battered by the fury of the waves; one moment raised upon a surging crest, the next in the trough of despair. He is in imminent danger of complete collapse, but finally the storm abates as he sees the way to recovery in the calmer waters of vengeance through the law.

Study the scene and read it aloud several times. The speech is in prose, yet there is rhythm. Movement is not smooth. It is the movement of storm, violent and thunderous. It rushes forward with tempestuous speed; it gathers momentum and then subsides. There are flashes of lightning which reveal the deepest emotions and thoughts, until finally it reaches a terrible calm, full of foreboding and a desperate purpose.

Words are the outward signs of inward thoughts. They are the result of thought; they are stimulated by the words of others as well as by our own thought. In this scene Shylock's mind and his speech are influenced and shaped by the words of Salarino and Tubal as well as by his own bitter thoughts.

The language in Act 2 of *Pygmalion* is very different from the language of Shakespeare, yet it reveals thought and character in a very similar way. The language is simple and direct, its rhythm varies with character and with the ideas expressed. Liza is alert and sharp, her speech is quick, positive, and incisive; Mrs. Pearce is prim and proper, her speech is calm and precise; the Colonel's speech is polished, correct, and commanding; while that of Professor Higgins is as varied as language itself.

Read the scene aloud and try to sense the variety of expression. Study particularly the speeches of Professor Higgins and notice how the sentences respond to thought. Considerable variety of pace, intensity, and tone are contained within the language. The rhythm of speech changes as Higgins addresses different people.

It follows his thought and his attitude towards the person addressed.

Speak the speech as Bernard Shaw has pronounced it to you. The eccentricity of Higgins towards Liza is not through a desire to be eccentric, but because he knows that his purpose in wanting her to stay in the house will not be understood by her whatever he says. He therefore uses language that a mere child could understand. It is simple, straightforward, and contains details in which a child would be interested, even though it is exaggerated, fantastic, and even absurd. Liza, as the Professor expects, believes literally what he has said, and states categorically that she does not want to do any of the things he suggests. The scene is great fun if the actors speak the speeches as set down with proper regard to rhythm, meaning, and purpose.

Speech for the actor is not similar to that of the reciter. An actor is never a reciter, no matter how long a speech may be. He is always part of something greater than himself. His speeches contribute to a dialogue or conversation. What he has to say may be declamatory or even oratorical, but it always bears some relation to other parts of the dialogue or to other characters. In other words, the actor is always concerned with dramatic speech or dialogue.

Apparent Naturalism

In the modern play, set within the four walls of a room, there is naturally a tendency for dialogue to approximate more nearly towards conversation. There is the suggestion that the characters are talking as ordinary people do talk within their own rooms. This apparent naturalism sometimes leads to unfortunate results on the stage, especially when amateurs and less experienced professionals are concerned. In an effort to appear natural, the true purpose of the dialogue is missed, with the inevitable result that the audience has little interest in what is going on.

Turn to the Chorus to Act 1 of James Bridie's *A Sleeping Clergyman*. How should either Cooper or Coutts be played? This scene is not one of the most important in the play, and generally these parts are given to inexperienced players who are told: "You haven't got much to do; it won't take up much of your time." It is unfortunate, too, that the more important parts of the play demand so much time at rehearsal that this and also the Chorus to Act 2 probably receive little attention from the producer. Should the statement "You haven't much to do" be accepted, or should the fact be faced that a part has to be performed and that something must be made of it? I suggest the latter, for I know that from a careful study of small parts a lot of fun can be obtained and considerable valuable experience gained in the art of acting.

Readily we can see that the whole scene represents the gossip of a club room, but in the main it is gossip with a difference. There is considerable chatter, but there is also a degree of reminiscence which is more for the benefit of the audience than it is for either Coutts or Cooper. From this dialogue we can see the reason for being on the stage, and this is half-way to knowing how they have to speak. Bridie tells us the kind of men they are: both are well educated, both belong to the medical profession, and both know the same people, although one of them has a very poor memory which has continually to be jogged. This is obviously an artificial device to enable Bridie and the actors to bring before the audience those subjects they should be interested in, namely, the Sleeping Clergyman and the Day of Judgment, Dr. Marshall, and, more particularly, the Camerons. Speech must direct attention to these important features. Dialogue is for the most part crisp, even jerky, and in contrast to the final speech, which is the climax of this little scene and the introduction to the play itself. This dogmatic speech concludes with: "Marshall was always a bit of a lame-dog fancier," which tersely sums up the character of Marshall as we shall see him throughout the play.

This scene is not easy for beginners, but it can be an interesting study in speech. The dialogue of the modern play is rarely easy to speak, for each sentence, which is frequently a whole speech, is packed with meaning, significance, and character.

Read Act 1, Scene 1, of this same play, and try to hear in your mind the sound of the speech as the scene moves towards its climax. Try to visualize the various persons as they come and go. Listen to the direct and forthright speech of Mrs. Hannah, sometimes shocked and sometimes angry, frequently puzzled, and even horrified. A kindly, but sorely tried, soul if ever there was one, and garrulous, too, given a chance. And kindly Dr. Marshall, what of his speech? His language expresses competence as well as kindliness, there are firmness of purpose and painstaking persuasiveness. He is at once a medical adviser and a kindly friend. His speech is sometimes blunt, almost brutally so, and it can be soothing; at the same time, when he is out of his intellectual depths, he is intolerant and scornful. He can be charitable towards the most depraved individual, but

new ideas which he cannot understand rouse him to
anger and bitter comment. It is worth noting that
Cameron speaks of Marshall's beautiful voice and his
bright and breezy manner.

Listen to the speech of poor Harriet, Marshall's
young sister, as it reveals her tragic disillusionment.
The simple, short sentences, the staccato phrases, are
tossed from a mind tortured and tottering, as the character of her lover becomes clearer in her mind. Here
are simplicity and passion. There is confidence born
of love, and terrible anger wrought from a mind dis-
traught and unbalanced. Her bitterness is expressed in
language which lashes and cuts deep into the flesh and
mind of Cameron. Her moods do not move forward
easily or smoothly; they vacillate from one to another,
and her speech responds to each conflicting desire and
emotion.

And now for our final study in this scene: the speech
of Cameron himself; the speech of the scientific
genius, the man who is on the threshold of an epoch-
making discovery and whose proofs are already near
completion, in the test-tubes arranged on the table;
the low debauchee, drunkard, false lover and friend, the
arrogant bully, and self-sufficient sponge. Listen to his
enthusiastic, excited, yet controlled speech as he
describes his scientific ideas and discoveries. Listen to
the speech of the scientific pioneer, logical and prophetic,
excited and exultant. Listen to the fighter who faces
death, and accepts its challenge but not its victory until
the moment when he sees the proofs of his discoveries
destroyed. His speech reveals the lowest and meanest
kind of creature, but it also reveals a mind which may
one day be acclaimed for its great work on behalf of

mankind. As we listen we are bewildered by the complexity of such a being. But the Clergyman sleeps on, the Day of Judgment has not come.

This is not the simple language of everyday life. It is not the recording of language with which we are familiar in our dealings with our neighbours. Cameron is not a character we meet regularly in our daily round. Yet it is life-like, even though its dimensions are greater in every way than those with which we are commonly in contact. We have, perhaps, never met a genius face to face, and, thank goodness, we have never been in close contact with such a low-down character as Cameron. Yet we must see him whole, and act him whole, even though we don't like him. We must see the visionary, the poet-scientist, as well as the creature which fills us with disgust. Speech must measure up to character. It must possess the range to reveal the full scope of intellect and emotion, and it must have the passion which alone can portray the excitement of both the struggle and the achievement.

A study of this scene will naturally bring realization that closely associated with speech is movement, for it is clearly not possible to visualize these people merely as talking puppets. Indeed, the climax of this scene is intimately connected with the movement of Harriet which destroys the test-tubes containing the precious evidence of Cameron's discoveries and experiments. It has been convenient to consider speech as something separate, but one is always conscious that vocal expression, movement, and gesture are but details of a single interpretation.

CHAPTER III

SUIT THE ACTION TO THE WORD

MOVEMENT is a condition of the theatre. It is not something imposed by actors, but is a necessary condition of drama and the acting space, that is, the stage.

When critics of the Victorian theatre railed against movement and gesture, they did not suggest that acting should be static. They demanded that these vital necessities should be controlled and rational. Their strictures opposed the extravagant, unrelated gestures and the artificial movement that contributed little or nothing to proper interpretation. Gesture they asserted should be relevant to the situation and to the purpose of the character and the play.

Movement is one of the immediate problems of the actor. On the open stage of the Elizabethans all characters had to enter; in the modern theatre, only a limited number is "discovered" on the stage when the curtain rises.

"Enter" is a simple instruction, but is it really so in practice? What does it actually imply and impose?

"Enter" is an instruction to the actor to emerge from his own world into that of the author; to become part of the make-believe world presented to the audience. At this moment he ceases to be himself and assumes the characteristics, physical and mental, of the being he represents. At this moment he begins to act.

"When do I go on?" is a common question. The actor would be better advised to ask: "How shall I go on?" To answer, he must know what impression he wishes to make upon the audience. This impression must be made immediately, and, therefore, what he does, and how he does it, are of the greatest importance, and call for the greatest care. The actor is at once brought up against the problems of deportment, walking, and sometimes running. In the modern play he is frequently concerned with the opening and closing of doors, with carrying trays, and even, on occasion, small tables. These may seem relatively unimportant when set against the major tasks of acting, yet they give "finish" to a performance or, when done indifferently, they cause considerable confusion and create undesirable effects.

Deportment

The problem of deportment is never unimportant. It establishes an aspect of personality. The manner in which a character "carries" himself may be an indication both of his background and of his character. Bill Crichton and Colonel Pickering carry themselves with dignity natural to their respective professions; the poise of Mrs. Higgins is in contrast to the slovenly ways of Liza Doolittle. In the final Act of *Pygmalion* the dustman, Doolittle, is dressed-up in frock-coat, white waistcoat, and grey trousers ready to go to his wedding at St. George's, Hanover Square. He presents a comic figure, and his entrance is greeted with laughter, because neither his character nor his general manner suits his get-up. This is a legitimate case of not suiting the action to the word.

Entrance

The actor must "suit the action to the word" on his entry, just as he must at all other times.   If he is excited, he must show it by his manner of coming on; if he is depressed, he must show depression at once; his way of coming into any scene must vary according to the character portrayed.

In addition to knowing how he will enter, an actor must also know where he is going when he emerges in front of the footlights: where he is going, and how he will get there.   This, of course, is perhaps more the concern of the producer than it is of the actor.   Yet when the producer has done his part, it is the actor who has to carry out the job.

In the last scene of *Twelfth Night* Sebastian suddenly rushes into the scene.   He is in a hurry to join his newly-married wife and to explain to her why he has hurt her kinsman.   His anxiety causes him to ignore the presence of others, until strange comment by Duke Orsino causes him to realize that he has become the centre of attention.

This is an interesting entrance because it contains several problems that do normally affect entrances. There is reason for the hurried entrance in the language of Sebastian.   It also explains where he will go when he enters, and indicates the speed at which he will speak to Olivia.   Soon, however, the language reveals that he does not get the kind of reception he had anticipated, and at once there is forced upon him a change of attitude, movement, and manner of speech.   Thus, there is the reminder that an actor must find out why he has to enter, what is the dramatic purpose in bringing him into the scene, and what he may expect from others already on the stage.

Principles that apply to Shakespeare's plays apply equally to modern plays, although realistic scenery may affect technical details. The opening and closing of doors not only give the actor movements that must be allowed for and rehearsed, but they also create a tendency to retard movement, unless the author provides a servant to announce the entrance of a particular character.

Realistic scenery is often a handicap to amateurs who have little scope to rehearse with the actual set. For this reason amateurs are far better served by either curtain or screen sets.

When Shylock is about to enter in the Trial Scene of *The Merchant of Venice* the Duke says: "Make room and let him stand before our face." This is an instruction that clearly affects a number of characters. The entrance of Shylock involves a whole group in movement. Those already on the stage have to move to make room for Shylock and in such a way that he may take his proper place before the Duke. These movements raise the problem of co-ordination which may be resolved artistically only by careful planning and precise rehearsal.

In *Reunion*, a one-act play by W. St. John Tayleur, there is an interesting entrance to study. The silent entrance of "The Figure," which interrupts the conversation of those who have just finished the reunion dinner, presents problems both for the player who enters and for all those already on the stage. The entrance itself is quiet and almost unperceived. There is mystery here, for the audience do not know who the

character is.   He is an intruder and as such he is immediately greeted.   He knows he is an intruder, even
after those on the stage have mistakenly identified him
as their old comrade whose efforts years ago had saved
their lives.   He was supposed to be dead, but here he
is alive and looking well.   He alone knows that they
have mistaken him for his dead brother.   On his entry
he had not meant to deceive, but to introduce himself
as the brother of their dead comrade.   The conversation
overheard at his entrance and the general appearance of
affluence and self-satisfaction caused him to allow the
deception to continue.

The actual entrance of "The Figure" clearly concerns
deportment and demeanour.   Immediately he is seen
there must be awareness that he is to dominate the scene;
that he brings into the room the dignity of an observer
and a mystery that time alone can solve.   His movement
will be slow, quiet, and dignified.   His gaze will be
upon those around the table.   It will be steady and
thoughtful.   There will gradually develop a slight
frown.   For the others, movement will be sudden and
expressive, first of resentment, and then of enthusiastic
welcome.   Their movements will portray excitement,
pleasure, and astonishment, mixed with an uncertainty
that in one character is slow to disappear.

Look at the comings and goings of the characters in
Act 3 of *Pygmalion* and notice how the various arrivals
of the Eynesford Hills, Colonel Pickering, and especially
of Liza Doolittle, affect the movements of those already
in the drawing-room.   Notice the effect of Liza's exit
on both the movements and the positions of the other
characters.   The scene is never still; movement
throughout plays its part.

Movement and Gesture

Movement and gesture are part of character. They
reveal the mood and the thoughts of characters as
surely as the spoken word. The characters of Shakespeare and Dickens emphasize the truth of this. Modern
plays are in no way different, except in degree. The
costume and manners of to-day naturally impose movement different from that of the Elizabethan or the "cloak
and dagger" period, but there are still movements that
are elegant, emotional, slovenly, careless, alert, and quick.

Turn again to the speeches by Gratiano and Enobarbus
(Chapter II) and think of them from the point of view
of movement and gesture. Gratiano is far more lively
and restless than Enobarbus. His character and his
speech demand movement. Gesture must be suited to
character and not to actual words. The hands must
not be employed to indicate the position of either the
liver or the wrinkles. The movement of hands, arms,
and of the whole body should be broad and bold to
suit the restless gaiety of this jolly companion. Enobarbus, on the other hand, is sober and restrained, his
purpose being to direct attention to what he has to say
about Cleopatra.

In the production of *The Happy Marriage* the beautiful
movement and gesture, especially of the hands, of Miss
Kay Hammond were wonderful and charming. The
actress moved with the grace and rhythm of a dancer.
The intricate and delicate pattern of movement was
arrested only by poses that emphasized moments of
special dramatic and humorous purpose. Her movements at once enchanted the audience and revealed the
character.

These movements, however, are not for imitation. They are her personal creation; part of the expression of her personality, and so are woven into the character interpreted.

Herein lies one of the difficulties of movement and gesture. They cannot be imposed upon the actor. There is never one special set of actions for a particular speech or character. *The actor must solve for himself the problem of gesture. He must create the pattern and drill himself until it becomes a rhythmic part of his being.*

Although gesture cannot be imposed, an actor cannot dispense with it merely because he thinks it unnecessary or because he cannot find or perform suitable gestures. Further, because a gesture is natural to the actor, it is not necessarily suitable for the stage or the character. There is appropriateness on the stage; and that which may be appropriate in ordinary life may be inappropriate for the character the actor is playing. This applies not only to the movements of such characters as Gratiano and Sir Andrew Aguecheek, Uriah Heep and Micawber, Hamlet and Macbeth, but also to the characters in modern plays.

Those who saw Sir Gerald Du Maurier will recall how he toyed with a lady's necklace, or opened a cigarette case, took out a cigarette and lit it during an intimate conversation. These simple movements were made with care and precision, and woven into the pattern of the scene. They gave poise and truth to his performance. They were not suited to words, but to the characters played, and the situations in which they figured. They were practised until they appeared to be spontaneous and natural. They were part of Du Maurier, but he made them part of his characters. They possessed charm, poise, and significance.

Movement must be significant. It must be part of character, or related to language or emotion. It may be bold and free, or restrained, even sparse. This will depend on character and language.

In great contrast to the free-flowing movement of Miss Hammond in *The Happy Marriage* was the stodgy, almost immobile, figure of Mr. Michael Shepley. His movement was restricted to a minimum; his hands moved only when called upon to perform a specific manual task. His whole being was firm and rigid. He was immovable and fixed, the complete antithesis of agility, both mentally and physically. He set the seal upon his character immediately he entered, and retained throughout the stodgy, unimaginative, unemotional, and somewhat bewildered figure of George Foster. The character hadn't an idea in his head, speech was limited to simple ejaculations, and his movement was restricted to the purely utilitarian moving of chairs and the turning on and off of a wireless set. The portrayal was a performance of controlled and effective immobility; a figure of delightful fun; an endearing fool.

My Lady's Dress, by Edward Knoblock, is an excellent play for amateurs with scenes in which characters of various nationalities and social background are represented. Problems in movement and gesture arise out of costume, period, nationality, and character. In the Dutch scene the gesture of the arrogant young fop, Jankheer Ian, is at once artificial, elegant, and exaggerated. Gesture shows off his personal figure as well as his wonderful attire, with its laces and frills. Movements for the whole body, especially of hands, arms, and legs, must be planned and co-ordinated until they present a rhythmic pattern of elegance and significance. The movement, planned as a dance, is artificial. It is imposed by the character of the young man whose conceit and taste combine to establish his manners and his affectations. Set against his extravagant style are the natural beauty and charm of the young girl who pretends to be a saleswoman.

In contrast is the scene of the dingy room in the East End peopled by a group of very poor cockneys. Movement and gesture are as cramped as both the room itself and that imposed upon the little cripple girl who is its central figure. The characters are homely, and gesture is limited by the situation and the household tasks performed.

In contrast, again, there is the ultra-fashionable showroom at Jacquelin's dress salon. Here are colour and display. A mannequin parade is in progress. Its purpose is to show off dresses. This imposes movement. It is a drill which is artificially elegant, stylized, and graceful. Mannequins move about the stage so that both those on the stage and in the audience are able to inspect the dresses. The girls look happy and resplendent. Their job is to sell and they must seem to enjoy what they do. They must attract attention, especially of the men who are the actual prospective buyers. But below this veneer is the real person: the cockney, the discontented, and the sensitive. The movement and the appearance of these girls are shams which deceive, which are planned to deceive. Among the customers, too, there are elegant and over-dressed beings whose dialogue reveals that they, too, are shams, that they also display a front very different from that which lies

THE GLOBE THEATRE, BANKSIDE, 1616

behind the facade of gentility and fashion. Their movement and gesture are also artificial and imposed. Indeed, all are shams in the world of *My Lady's Dress*.

Consider movement in the first act of *The Sleeping Clergyman*. Look upon the tortured body of Cameron as the scene opens. He is in bed, his body wracked by a terrible cough. He is suffering both bodily and mentally because his illness obstructs him in his work, which is more to him than health. Think about his dialogue with Harriet, and visualize the movements as the dialogue proceeds. Both are highly wrought by conflicting emotions, and movement responds to the varying moods and emotions. There is a crescendo of movement, just as there is a crescendo of emotion. Indeed, the one corresponds to the other, and it is the climax of movement that brings about the climax in the emotional strain and the climax of the scene itself. Think also about the movement during the dialogue between Cameron and Marshall. It is more dignified and restrained, yet very tense as Cameron reveals his scientific vision. The movement throughout this scene varies with character and emotional stress.

Movement must be studied and precise; purposeful and controlled. Here lies a paradox. In life, movement would be uncontrolled as Harriet's passion is uncontrolled. She would lose grip on both thought and action. What she does would be entirely spontaneous and a direct result of her feelings. All would be unpremeditated and irrational. On the stage, however, everything she does must be under complete control, preconceived, planned, rehearsed, and co-ordinated with the movements of Cameron. Nothing must be left to chance.   Accurate timing will give an appearance of spontaneity.

In many Broadway theatres, especially when the play is slight in structure and purpose, there is a tendency for movement to become an imposed adornment rather than a direct result of the need for interpretation.   On the stage there is displayed appropriate furniture, but this is not always used for its legitimate purpose. Characters certainly do sit on chairs, but only for brief moments.   Then, for no apparent reason, they are whisked away to another part of the stage, perhaps to sit again in a new position.   This restlessness is, perhaps, due to the influence of the cinema in which the camera as well as the actors are for ever on the move.   Similar restlessness in individual gesture is also displayed by many actors.   Often both movements and gestures are as extravagant as were those of earlier days that aroused serious critics to bitter comment.   One explanation is that many plays are so slight that but for these adornments and graces there would be little to appeal to audiences.   In such plays the actor becomes the centre of interest, almost the only interest.   Such plays should not be attempted by amateurs.

The Ability to "Look"

Too often amateurs, and, indeed, the less skilled professionals, give little thought to movement and gesture.   Hands are unmeaning appendages of the arms; eyes, which have been described as the "windows of the soul," express little but vacancy; and general deportment remains completely unrelated to character and thought alike.   It is true that speech is of first importance in the theatre, but it is also true that an effect

created by speech can be marred and ruined by bad and
ill-thought-out gesture, by careless movements of
hands, body, and eyes. These are, too, frequent causes
of distraction and irritation. The whole body must be
disciplined to do the actor's bidding.

In Act 2 of *Berkeley Square* there is an episode in
which Peter Standish and Helen gaze into each
other's eyes and Helen sees the future through the eyes
of Peter. It is a dramatic episode of intense "looking"
at and into the eyes of the other. The gesture must
be held during speech and provide the reason for speech.
It is by looking that Helen sees the things she describes,
and it is by the intensity of Peter's gaze that she is able
to see those things.

The ability to "look" on the stage frequently baffles
amateurs. The eyes, like the tongue, are difficult to
control and focus. They have a marked tendency to
rove, and the roving eye is mischievous. It is often the
mark of the flirt, the deceiver, the irresponsible, and the
nit-wit. On the stage this restlessness of the eyes is
frequently due to the fact that the actor does not know
what he has to look at, and consequently he looks up
at the "flies," or gazes at the floor, or intermittently
glances into the audience. The actor must cultivate
the habit of looking at people or things on the stage.
By this manner of "seeing," an audience is told whether
the object seen is familiar or strange, of intense or merely
passing interest.

Peter Standish, newly arrived in eighteenth-century
London from the twentieth century, looks upon all he
meets with the inquisitive and inspecting gaze of an
antiquary, until he sees Helen. At once her beauty and
quiet demeanour claim his attention; he ceases to be an

antiquarian, and his eyes reveal only tenderness. He is spellbound by this unexpected vision. Hitherto his eyes have asked questions; now they give something in exchange for the feelings that the discovery has brought to him. In his eyes Helen sees at once the message of affection, and so does the audience. This brief moment is of considerable dramatic importance and significance.

Eyes reveal thought and feeling; the dreamer and the visionary. They interpret passion and sympathy.

Co-ordination of the movements of all parts of the body presents great difficulty; yet it is of considerable importance. Uriah Heep and Bill Crichton rub their hands together as if washing them, but this is the only habit they possess in common. Uriah Heep is furtive and shifty in his gaze; Crichton open and direct; Heep stoops and cringes; Crichton is upright and manly in his bearing. The smile and speech of Heep express the fawning sycophant; the speech and gravity of Crichton, confidence and helpfulness. Wholeness of movement and gesture gives verisimilitude to interpretation.

Movement and gesture should be born from the play itself, from its characters, and from its language. The suggestion that movement should be natural is a meaningless phrase. Natural to what and to whom? Movement and gesture natural to a cockney are not so natural to an army colonel; gesture natural to a Frenchman is not similar to that of a Chinese; gesture and movement suitable for a naturalistic play will not suit Shakespearian drama or the comedy of manners.

Passion, Poison, and Petrifaction, by Bernard Shaw, provides an exciting exercise in exaggerated movement. Shaw described the play as "A Brief Tragedy For Barns and Booths." His mention of barns and booths carries the mind back to an era of acting and drama of which the present generation knows nothing, except what it may read or gather from old prints. It was an age that revelled in melodrama such as *Maria Marten* and in acting of a vigorous, broad, and exaggerated style. It was the "cloak and dagger" period, in which the villain was hearty and jovial.

Shaw's play is fantastic, absurd, but when it is played with appropriate movement and vigour is riotously funny. The villain of the piece is the husband of Lady Magnesia. He enters in evening dress over which he wears a crimson cloak, carrying a broad dagger. Stealthily, he moves toward the bed on which lies his wife, whose life is saved by a sudden sneeze.

I will not spoil the plot by detailing it here. Read it and visualize the characters as they move about the room and speak the exaggerated language.

Shaw created an absurd world, but if we accept it, we must also accept his characters and their story. Their speech, movements, and dress are of a special convention. Within that convention they are real and living. They must be visualized as sincere, serious beings. They do not think themselves "funny" in any way, and they must not be played as such. They do what they do because it is natural to them in their special world.

Lady Magnesia's sneeze saved her life, but nothing so propitious comes between the villain and his wife's lover, who drinks from the poisoned tumbler to the accompanying mocking laughter of the husband. The lover is, however, saved from death, but worse is to follow.

This is a play of studied movement and gesture for each character, combined with flamboyant language that aptly fits the characters and their fantastic world.

Movement Must be Selected and Arranged

In *The Plays for Dancers* by W. B. Yeats, a special stylized movement is imposed by both the mythological figures and the beautiful masks that they wear. The characters are super-human, and Yeats makes them wear masks to differentiate them from humans. The producer must arrange movement to emphasize their character and to retain the beauty of the masks. It will have the rhythm of dance, but be a selected kind of special dance to assist in the interpretation of character and play. It will not be extravagant, but, as with the mask, something imposed upon the actor. It will be movement removed from anything that suggests the present, either in place or in time. It will, indeed, suggest remoteness, dignity, and grace.

In T. S. Eliot's *Murder in the Cathedral* a Chorus actually becomes an additional character, but not a "natural" character. Its introduction is an artifice of dramatic technique, a powerful force, but none the less something arbitrarily imposed. The Chorus speaks as a choir, not always in unison, not always all together, but yet as a distinctive unit. Each individual is only a part of a whole, but generally the individuals speak together. We do hear an individual as well as a crowd, but each individual's voice gives articulation to thoughts that belong to the crowd itself. This crowd is not static, nor is it a body set on the side of the stage or apart from the action. It moves into the scene itself and becomes part of it. How does it move? Is each member given a free hand to move naturally as she thinks right or feels urged to do? Obviously not. Such a method would produce chaos. Both individual movements

and the movement of the united body have to be
arranged and rehearsed with great care. There must
be variety of movement to suggest individual personality
and to respond to varied emotion and urgency. This
chorus, however, must not be confused with an ordinary
crowd. It is different from either the crowd in *Julius
Caesar* which listens to Antony's oration, or the crowd
which listens to John Shand in *What Every Woman
Knows*. It is not a group of separate individuals brought
naturally together, but a group introduced by an artificial device to carry out a specific dramatic purpose
imposed upon it by the dramatist. The individuals in
the Chorus have personality, but not as the individuals
in the crowd addressed by Marullus. They are called
Women of Canterbury, but, actually, they are the Voices
of the Human Mass of all places and all times. Movement for such a body should be stylized to emphasize
the intensity of human suffering and appeal, and to differentiate it from the real figures of Becket and the rest.
When simple human and natural movements are given
to the Chorus much of its verbal dignity and purpose is
reduced to insignificance.

On the Victorian stage movement and gesture tended
to become stereotyped and conventional. The actor
knew that he must conform to the "unities" of movement, and he used special gestures for particular emotions. He knew how to show fear, horror, contempt.
The villain moved with bold extravagant gestures, and
was always recognizable, not only by his get-up but
also by the green light that followed him round the
stage. However, all actors of this period did not mis-
use their art. Sir Henry Irving was a great actor.
Though few theatregoers of to-day saw him, they have

A dramatic scene from T. S. Eliot's "Murder in the Cathedral," produced at the University Theatre, University of Chicago.

Courtesy ANTA

This production of "Murder in the Cathedral," is by the Carolina Playmakers at the University of North Carolina, Chapel Hill, N. C.

Courtesy ANTA

heard his praises, and in *Henry Irving* E. Gordon Craig
tells of his work and the great hold he had on the
theatregoing public. His detailed description of Irving's
first entrance as Mathias in *The Bells* is a most instructive
passage, recalling the great actor at work as the elaborate
and intricate pattern of movement develops.

Movement is precise and rhythmic. The invention of
gesture follows, and is inspired by the thoughts of a
tormented man, by the spoken words of those around
him, and by the emotions that rush in upon him.
Movement is slow, deliberately slow, and there are
many significant pauses as the whole moves consciously
and painstakingly towards its climax. Fingers, hands,
eyes, and the whole body play their allotted parts in this
amazing and moving scene.

Irving deliberately not only suited the action to the
word but also to the thoughts and emotions that
they aroused. His invention was purposeful in its
significance. Everything was rehearsed to have the
maximum effect on the minds of the audience. It was
conscious and deliberate art, timed and planned to the
minutest detail. Yet, it was economic, for no gesture
or movement was extravagant or irrational.

Irving did not use gesture for gesture's sake, or to
illustrate unnecessarily. The slow, revolving movement of Irving's head, the gradual straightening of his
body, and the steady gaze of his eyes were inspired by
words and thoughts, and were not merely illustrations
of them. Movement did not merely repeat what had
been said and understood; it added something of
significance.

Perhaps the most important lessons to be learnt by
amateurs and many professionals from details of Irving

at work are that gesture and movement must be deliberately planned and purposeful.   Careless, uncontrolled gesture, and uncertain movement that lacks precision, add nothing of value to interpretation and are irritating to an audience.   The Victorian stage was over-elaborate and fussy.   To-day there is frequently a careless disregard of proper effects that is disturbing. Too much is left to chance feelings and inspiration where none is inspired.

CHAPTER IV

INTERPRETATION OF CHARACTER

THE proper study of the actor is the play. The great French actor, Coquelin, said: "When I have to create a new role, I begin by reading the play with the greatest attention, five or six times. First, I consider what position my character should occupy, on what plane in the picture I must put him. Then I study his psychology, knowing what he thinks and what he is morally. I deduce what he ought to be physically, what will be his carriage, his manner of speaking, his gesture. These characteristics once decided, I learn the part without thinking about it further. Then when I know it, I take up my man again, and closing my eyes I say to him: 'Recite this for me.' Then I see him delivering the speech, the sentence I asked him for; he lives, he speaks, he gesticulates before me, and then I have only to imitate him."

Thus, for Coquelin, acting was imitating a mental image of a character, formed from a close study of the play. This mental image was so vivid that for him it was actually a living being, moving, speaking, gesticulating; one that he could see, feel, and hear; one that would perform at his command.

All actors and actresses can study with similar eagerness and purpose, and deduce from dialogue the various physical and mental details of characters, but it is not so certain that all can form such intense mental images.

For many visual images are far more vivid than auditory ones. The mental image of the way in which a character speaks may be far more illusive than that of the manner in which he moves or gesticulates. It is possible to know what a character is morally, but difficult, even impossible, to feel and think as the character does.

The literary scholar searches for knowledge about the play and its characters. He analyses and explains; describes and criticizes. Dramatic critics can tell all about a character, but cannot necessarily interpret it to an audience. It does not even follow that because they know all there is to know about a character they possess any clear mental images of the physical and mental qualities of it. They may not see the character as a living being, but rather as a specimen to be dissected, examined, described, and explained.

The actor undoubtedly dissects, but having done so he must build up the character again. He, too, analyses in order that he may understand, but after analysis he must assemble the details so that the character becomes whole again in his mind. He needs not only to know the separate aspects of it, but also to see the character moving and speaking as a living being. He deduces from the play "what he ought to be physically, what will be his carriage, his manner of speaking, his gesture," and then builds these separate things into an image of a complete living being.

The building-up of mental images is not a simple task. The ability to build does not come automatically; it must be developed. Whenever a play is read, efforts should be made to visualize the characters in motion. This involves reading the play with attention, perhaps several times. Coquelin said he read a play five or six

times.   This clearly means that even for one as experienced as he, the task demanded considerable effort.   He
was not satisfied with a mere introduction to the character; he needed to know him fully.

One way of developing the power to visualize is by
comparing one character with another.   It is for this
reason that in Chapters I and II various characters were
considered together.   The characteristics of one character are heightened when they are seen against those of
another, especially when they differ greatly from one
another.

Naturally, some characters are more easily visualized
than others.   Indeed, some are so slightly sketched by the
dramatist that they almost defy visualization.   Rosen-
crantz and Guildenstern, Salarino and Salanio, are examples of Shakespearian characters that possess little to
distinguish one from the other.   They are unrewarding
parts for the actors.   On the other hand, there are many
small parts that bring great reward when they are performed with imagination and invention.   The Clowns
in *A Midsummer Night's Dream* are a wonderful collec-
tion.   Simply drawn, they are simple folk.   Each is a
distinctive being, even though all are not equally important.   For the interpretation of such characters the
actor needs to invent action and by-play.

By-play is a legitimate, and sometimes an essential,
part of interpretation.   It should not, however, be
imposed upon a scene merely to create an effect.   It
should be welded into the scene and into the characterization so that it has the appearance of spontaneity.

Bully Bottom and his Athenian friends form themselves into an amateur dramatic society.   Their
intention is to perform a play before the Duke and his

Duchess on their wedding night. They are to play the tragedy of "Pyramus and Thisby." They know nothing about acting. All except Bully Bottom are quite aware of this fact, but they are not daunted by their ignorance. Bully Bottom will carry them through. He will make them famous. He will move the audience to tears and make the Duke applaud and reward them for their wonderful effort. Their performance is truly "wonderful." Bottom carries all before him. His effort is sheer "virtuosity." He blazes his way through with delightful bombast, and kills himself most valiantly. Not for him the task of visualizing Pyramus; he cares nothing for him. The only character Bottom cares about is himself, and he plays that most admirably. He learns his words, dons helmet and sword, and delivers himself with vigour and enthusiasm. He takes the centre of the stage and keeps it, even in death. He and his friends do everything on the stage that actors should not do, but as they are blissfully ignorant of this it really does not matter, and everyone is happy.

Shakespeare provides many small parts that are worthy of study and most rewarding in performance. Amateurs who wish to improve should undertake as many of these parts as possible. Each will increase the player's ability to form mental images and develop the technical skill that is required to communicate interpretation to an audience.

Try to visualize such characters as Fluellen in *Henry V*, or Borachio in *Much Ado About Nothing*. Do not merely describe them. Try to form a picture of them in your mind until you feel an urge to play them; to see yourself walking the stage as Fluellen and talking to the King as his equal. Picture yourself whipping Pistol and making him eat a leek.   Fluellen is a dominating character, irascible and quick-tempered.

Bully Bottom could see himself playing only the lead.   He always wanted the "lion's" part, so that he could roar and make the audience say "let him roar again."   This is no way to become an actor.   An actor must prepare himself if he wishes to be the "lead."   He must prepare by making himself master of his art. Mastery is the reward of study and experience.   Small parts, especially in Shakespeare's plays, give scope to gain experience.

All players are not suited to play leading parts.   Many leading roles demand physical or vocal qualities that some do not possess.   All are not equipped to play romantic parts or heroic figures.   This fact needs to be faced by professional and amateur alike.   In the professional theatre it is common to find actors playing to "type."   They are cast for a similar type of character year after year.   Many weary of this.   They demand, not always successfully, to get away from type casting. Many are doomed never to play important parts, and their chief hope is to get a part in which they may achieve a limited success.

Many amateurs, too, will never be able to play the major roles in any kind of play, but they, at least, need not suffer the boredom of being cast to "type."   The matter is in their own hands.   They should join a society which performs Shakespeare's plays.

The modern play frequently has a small cast in which only two or three characters have much to do.   Such plays are interesting to the few, and give experience to only those who are important.   These plays may be good, but they do not provide the amateur with enough

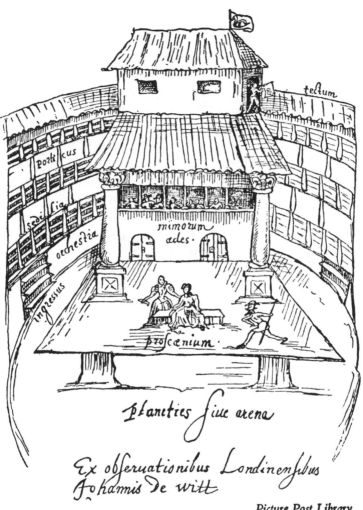

Picture Post Library

THE OLD SWAN THEATRE, BANKSIDE

Drawing showing the general conditions under which
Shakespeare's plays were originally produced

interest.   There are some modern plays with casts in which most of the characters are worth while, and which provide opportunity to others beside the leading characters.   These are the worth-while plays for the amateur.   In these there are suitable opportunities for many to practise the art of acting.   All may study the play and cultivate the necessary habit of forming mental images of character.

Read any play and try to form mental images of the characters; preferably choose a play not recently seen so that the mental images are not influenced by the memory of the voice and gesture of a particular actor or actress, for then the mental image may be of what has been seen and heard, and not of the characters.   This is most important, for it must be stressed that Coquelin's imitation was of the image formed directly from his study of the play, and not of another actor performing the part.

Imitation of Another is not Interpretation

Imitation inevitably directs attention to that which is imitated, and, consequently, leads thoughts away from the character being played.   It is irritating to see on either the amateur or the professional stage imitations of such actors as John Gielgud, Laurence Olivier, or Robertson Hare.   It may be true that imitation is the sincerest form of flattery, but often it is little short of impertinence.

Imagination and invention are qualities that actors and readers of plays should develop.   The novelist carefully describes his characters so that the reader sees them through his eyes.   The characters of Dickens and Scott are set before us as clearly as a portrait.   Frequently they are painted in words with as much detail as there is in a painting by Rembrandt. A dramatist does not supply such details. Both reader and actor must "deduce" from the play the details of carriage, gesture, manner of speech, and psychology. For the right deduction of these considerable intelligence, imagination, and invention are essential.

These qualities are necessary for the interpretation of every kind of character and play. The great plays of Shakespeare, Shaw, and other dramatists demand these qualities in full measure, but it is also true that without these qualities the simplest one-act plays cannot be performed with commendable success. Many of the one-act plays chosen by amateurs are little more than simple stories set in dialogue. Their author's sense of character is slight, and there is little differentiation between one character and another. Unfortunately, many amateurs or their advisers choose these plays because they, mistakenly, think they are easy to act. To make such plays live and make them effective in the theatre the actor must exercise considerable ingenuity and invention. These qualities are not usually possessed by beginners, and those who do possess them generally avoid such empty vehicles for expression.

Telling a story is not interpreting it. The teller of tales focuses attention on the tale he tells, not on himself as a character. His purpose is not to create interest in himself as a character, but in his story. Thus when dialogue is purely narrative and lacking in personality or character, the actor is redundant, for he is not essential to the narration. He is only a voice, even though the author gives him a courtesy name. For such plays to become interesting and effective in the theatre the actor must do the work that should have been done by the author: he must create personality and character.

When Coquelin and other actors have related how they "created" their roles, they have always insisted that, in one way or another, they searched in the play for the character that was created first by the author. They have not imposed character or personality upon dialogue, but have allowed character and personality to impose themselves on them. Indeed, in a great performance, it is true to say that the character has entered into the mind, body, and soul of the actor until they have become one.

It is true, of course, that actors have sometimes chosen plays in which they have been able to display their art, plays which would have had little significance or interest but for the great skill of the actor. Undoubtedly the skill of Henry Irving made the character of Mathias and *The Bells*; but his art, great as it was, did not create an interest either in *The Bells* or in the character. It aroused enthusiasm and controversy around the name of Irving, but it did not, however, involve discussion of the play or of its author.

Interpretation may be concerned with things other than character; for example, with ideas. There are plays in which character is subordinate to ideas, or, as in the plays of Shaw, where ideas and characters travel hand in hand. In such plays the actor has both to interpret character and to convey ideas. In spite of the importance of ideas expressed in Shaw's plays, and of much that the playwright said, interest in the theatre lies heavily on the side of character. *St. Joan* may illustrate what Shaw understood a genius to be, and discuss religious and political theories, but interest is focused on

the characters of Joan, the Earl of Warwick, the In-
quisitor, and many others. Shaw always created
character or, at least, outstanding personalities through
whom he delivered his ideas and his teaching. His
plays, like those of Shakespeare, Molière, Sheridan,
Galsworthy, Barrie, Priestley, and others, provide the
flesh and bones into which actors can breathe life.
Their plays provide material for theatrical interpretation,
for they contain those elements from which an actor can
"deduce" the physical, mental, and moral characteristics
of the being he is called upon to bring to life.

This word "deduce" which seems to creep un-
obtrusively into Coquelin's account of his method
should be considered.

Deduction is a logical and intellectual process. It is
the result of reason applied to facts, in this case obtain-
able from a play. Reason and logic concerned with
given data are not to be confused with feelings or
emotions. The source of Coquelin's inspiration,
according to his own account, was outside himself and
inside the play. Thus, when an actor is urged to give
from "within," he is really asked to give back what he
has taken into his mind and spirit from something outside himself. When he is unable to give from "within,"
it is usually because he has not devoted enough time or
thought to the study of the play itself, or deduced a
sufficiently clear image of the physical and mental
qualities of the character. His mental picture is
incomplete and unfinished.

Assimilation of Character

Acting from "within" is a result of the complete
assimilation of character. It is not a method of acting

that can be sought and trapped. It is the desired "something" which can follow only from efforts made upon material outside the mind of the actor. There should be no struggle or conscious effort to act from "within." It should result from relaxation, which is the hall-mark of all good acting. It implies comfort, ease, and a seeming naturalness. But relaxation itself is a result of effort, which, when achieved, gives assurance and ease to interpretation, and to the actor the appearance of being both natural and sincere in what he does.

Sincerity in acting is that quality which compels an actor to keep faith with author and audience. The dictionary definition is: "free from pretence or deceit." In one sense, therefore, it is paradoxical to apply the word to an actor, who must, by the nature of his work, pretend, and, consequently, deceive. Only when it is realized that an actor is an intermediary between author and audience does the word have any significance. An actor is sincere when he honestly and truthfully renders to an audience the character and ideas given to him in the play, for it is his duty to interpret these. He is insincere when he uses his role merely to display his own personality and ideas.

However, I do not suggest that an actor's personality is unimportant. On the contrary, it is one of his most precious gifts. An actor is a positive artist. He asserts with enthusiasm and assurance, and for the brief span of the play he imposes his will upon the minds of the audience. He must believe in himself and in what he does, be definite and authoritative. Uncertainty and hesitance in purpose or in method inevitably lead to confusion. In preparation he should be the modest inquirer, the painstaking seeker after information. He must search and question, struggle to clarify ideas and ways of interpretation, and be dissatisfied and self-critical. In performance, however, he must be self-assured, positive, and unhesitant. Only so can performance be truthful and convincing.

For interpretation an actor brings to his aid make-up and costume. Many actors have confessed that until they have used these aids they have not been entirely comfortable in their work. Others have stated that the right clothes and helpful make-up have done much to establish confidence. The amateur, unfortunately, has limited opportunities to study make-up under stage conditions, and frequently has to take whatever clothes are supplied or that he can afford. Many amateurs have their efforts ruined by the imposition of a beard, an ill-fitting wig, or by grease paint wrongly applied. Many appropriate gestures and movements are cramped or made ridiculous by an unmanageable costume or one that hangs from the shoulders like an ill-fitting sack. It is not my province to go into details of these important adjuncts to the actor's craft, but I strongly advise amateurs to use grease paint with moderation, and only to impose beards and wigs when it is impossible to do without them. I urge all to take special care to see that costumes fit, and that hats, cloaks, and capes are properly worn and managed. Make-up and costume should aid personality in the task of interpretation.

Much that I have said in previous chapters on speech and movement is concerned with the problem of interpretation. It has been convenient to deal with aspects of acting under separate headings, but in reality these are not separate. They function together, being inseparable partners of a single purpose. When a character has been completely visualized, speech and movement are the combined expression of that character. They are interdependent when the character lives, speaks, and gesticulates before an audience.

CHAPTER V

THE PLAY'S THE THING

A PLAY is a fiction conceived in the mind of a dramatist. The characters are of his choosing, they move against a background of his selection, and conflict as he determines. A play is not a haphazard world in which characters move with freedom and self-determination. It is a world where all is planned and co-ordinated, a world in which there are pattern and design.

A play is a single thing; characters, incidents, and ideas are parts of a whole, parts which illuminate and reveal the central theme and purpose of the play. Some parts may be of greater importance than others; some characters and incidents may stand out more clearly in the design; but no part may be greater than the whole. The play's the thing which has to be given life in the theatre.

It is natural that an actor should primarily be concerned with the interpretation of his own role. Nevertheless, he should see his character in its relation to other characters and to the design and purpose of the play. This relationship must be deduced as the play is studied, and before the final mental image of the character is created. One of the weaknesses of the actor-manager system, which ruled the theatre in the nineteenth century, was that actors frequently subordinated everything to their own histrionic desire. Great plays were used as vehicles for the display of their own skill, and plays of little merit were performed for no other reason than that they had parts which gave them opportunity to exhibit their personal abilities.

It is true that we frequently do go to a theatre to see a favourite actor, and that probably we should not go to see the play unless a particular actor or actress were playing. There can be no doubt about the attraction of the "Stars," but when these deliberately sacrifice the play on the altar of self-aggrandisement they do not serve the play or the theatre. It is true that we could not have *Hamlet* without the Prince, but it is also true that Hamlet's tragedy is concerned and conditioned by events and people beyond his control. The thoughts and actions of Hamlet's mother, uncle, and Ophelia are essential to the design of this great tragedy, and the performance of these parts and their relation to the development of the play must be observed.

The commercial theatre is sometimes apt to sacrifice truth in a performance in the belief that audiences will not accept it. An outstanding example of this was Sir Herbert Tree's production of *Twelfth Night*. Tree was convinced that the only way to win popular support for this comedy was by reliance on the mirth of Sir Toby Belch, Sir Andrew Aguecheek, Malvolio, and the Clown. He was sure the public could not be interested in the poetry or the romance. For a time events seemed to prove that he was right, for his production had a long run. The public certainly enjoyed the rough play of Toby and the ridiculous discomfiture of Malvolio. But all critics were not pleased, and early in the twentieth century forces were at work which ultimately proved that Tree was wrong, and that public taste was far more discerning than he had thought. In

1913 at the Savoy Theatre, London saw Granville-Barker's production of this same play in which all the elements of Shakespearian comedy received proper attention and were allotted their true relationships. Music, verse, romance, wooing, as well as the lively fun, were all given their place in the pattern of comedy. Verse was spoken with speed and regard for its cadences, song was welded into plot, and the background was simple and colourful. Character was interpreted with sincerity, and Malvolio was justly portrayed as a puritan steward, so that his downfall roused feelings of pity, not of ridicule. The production showed imagination and understanding; it proved the death knell to nineteenth-century methods of producing Shakespeare, and it was an outstanding example of "*The play's the thing.*"

It should be realized that audiences are capable of retaining only a limited number of impressions of what they see and hear. This makes it necessary for emphasis to be given to those moments which are directly concerned with the main purpose of a play. The play moves towards its climax, so does each scene and frequently each separate episode. These climaxes must be struck home if the play is to be understood. At these moments everybody on the stage must be under the greatest discipline; everything done must focus attention on the idea, emotion, or incident which is to be retained in memory. It is the producer's business to see that actors are aware of these climaxes; it is the actor's duty to see that he plays his allotted part.

The Happy Journey is an interesting and unusual play in which movement is important. The general manner and speech are realistic, but production calls for considerable imagination and invention. The background is a simple curtain and the stage is almost bare, as no particular place is being represented. The only furniture on the stage is a cot or couch and four chairs on a low platform arranged to suggest a motor-car. All other properties used by the actors are imaginary and must be suggested by mime.

The play presents the Kirby family on a visit by car to Camden, where a married daughter lives with her husband and baby. Members of the audience watch them make this journey in the "car" made-up of the four chairs.

A boy of 13 plays marbles, or rather mimes a game of marbles, before the journey starts. His sister, a girl of 15, talks to imaginary friends. They, together with their mother and father, are seen to get into the car and to drive away. The audience travels with them and participates in several adventures on the way. The opening and closing of the "car" doors have to be mimed; the starting of the "car" has to be suggested by the movements of the four sitting on the chairs representing the seats of the "car"; sudden stopping and starting call for special movements, as does the sudden swerving of the "car" to avoid an obstacle. All these movements must be controlled and co-ordinated with the greatest care and precision. They must be timed with accuracy, and rehearsed until they appear to be spontaneous and the direct result of the particular movement of the "car."

This miming is, however, but the background to the main purpose of the play, which is the portrayal of the character of Ma Kirby. She is the central figure of the comedy. Her humanity and good humour have to be brought home to the audience. The unusual setting and the miming are undoubtedly memorable. They provide fun and laughter. Above all, however, the character of Ma Kirby must dominate. She provides the purpose of the play, the living interest, the humanity; the rest is the background against which she lives and for whom she lives.

This is a "producer's" play. All the characters must submit to discipline, to the drill that the producer invents as he sets about his task of interpretation. The play is interpreted by a team under the control and guidance of a producer. Each character has a well-defined personality that must be established, but each must play as a cog in a machine, or, perhaps better, as a puppet on a skilfully controlled string. Even dominant Ma Kirby is always one of the team that travels along the road in the improvised "car."

Those who are responsible for the interpretation should remember that they are playing comedy, not farce. There will always be the possibility that eagerness to get laughs may obscure the essential purpose of the play. This danger must be avoided. The mime should be simple and purposeful; exaggeration should be avoided; the key-note should be "unobtrusiveness," for the "travelling" and the miming are but accompaniments to the character of the central figure.

This is a good play for amateurs because it impels study, calls for imagination and invention, demands discipline, and provides scope for individual interpretation and team-work.

Discipline is Essential on the Stage

Obviously, movements and stage positions must be controlled, but so also must the manner and style of acting. There must be single-minded production, with all working towards an agreed goal. Costumes must be in period, dialect must be uniform. Actors may not decide these things for themselves; they must conform to an agreed plan.

Even with regard to interpretation of character, the individual may not always be allowed to decide for himself. Actors do sometimes feel that they know better than the dramatist; they see themselves achieving greater success if they are allowed to perform in a way of their own choosing, instead of in the way indicated by the author. Actors should not attempt to secure success or "steal the limelight" at the expense of other characters or of the play.

The play is the only permanent thing in the theatre. All else is ephemeral. The Greek theatre lies in ruin, but Greek tragedy lives majestically in new surroundings; the "open" stage is now only a museum piece, but the plays of Shakespeare still dominate the world of drama; actors come and go, they strut their brief hour upon the scene and are forgotten or live vaguely in memory; stage carpenters, scenic artists, and electricians have their day and are cast aside. Only the play remains.

All plays, however, do not live. The majority pass into oblivion when their entertainment value ceases, and many die at birth, for they do not possess even this ephemeral quality. Plays should not be condemned because they entertain, for the theatre is a place of entertainment. Shaw wanted to use the theatre as a pulpit from which he could teach the public how to think and what to think, but he never forgot that the dramatist must entertain. For him the theatre was to be a substitute for the Church, but it was to be a Church in which laughter ruled, where joy was unconfined. But entertainment does not necessarily connote laughter. The mind may be entertained from diverse sources; and in the theatre entertainment may be provided by tragedy and tales of history as well as by comedy. For many the tragedies of Shakespeare may provide greater entertainment than the most modern farce, and the experiments of T. S. Eliot and Christopher Fry may give more satisfaction, emotionally and intellectually, than the realistic plays of their contemporaries.

Choosing a Play

The choosing of plays for performance is a problem which always presents difficulties. It faces the professional and the amateur. But the problem for these bodies is not the same. The professional is bound by conditions which do not affect the amateur. His choice is more circumscribed; he must have an eye on the box office, for the livelihood of many people is concerned. The amateur is bound to no one; he has only himself to please; he has freedom and, therefore, scope for experiment.

The amateur movement is not a single thing in which all concerned are moved by similar ideas and purposes. Moreover, it is not scientifically co-ordinated. Indeed, truly speaking it is not a movement at all.

Amateurs vary in ability and aims. There are those who act merely for fun, and those, the real amateurs, who love drama and cultivate the art of acting in order that they may interpret with understanding and sensibility.

There is nothing wrong in acting just for fun; it is quite a good way of spending leisure. These players do no harm either to themselves or to their friends. Sometimes they display considerable skill, which, combined with enthusiasm, provides entertainment and pleasure both for themselves and those who witness their performances. Their efforts should not be condemned, even though they do not call for high appraisement.

The true amateur, however, cultivates the art of acting. Cultivation implies effort to understand and to achieve. He is a student as well as a practitioner. He studies the conditions of the art and endeavours to improve and to achieve as a performer. Such players set their own standard, for they know their aim which is the interpretation of the work of the dramatist.

There is only one standard for the actor. Basically, one cannot suggest that a professional should act in one way, and an amateur in another. Nevertheless, while there is only one standard for the actor, there are clearly many different standards of acting: the standard of acting at a repertory theatre is not identical with that at the Memorial Theatre, Stratford-on-Avon, or at the best Broadway theatres. The standard of some professional acting is high, and there is also some professional acting that is very poor indeed.

Recognition of this is important because it is frequently reported that an amateur was "up to professional standard." Such a comment carries the implication that there is a definite meaning to be attached to the term "professional standard," when clearly there is none. There is neither a professional standard nor an amateur standard.

Acting is good when it interprets faithfully and sincerely, commands attention, and holds interest. The amateur is not in competition with the professional. He should not be his imitator, but an actor in his own right, performing in the way that he knows best and to the best of his ability. Immediately he steps on to the stage he is an actor—whether amateur or professional does not matter—an actor endeavouring to bring his character to life in the theatre. His work should not be measured by an imagined "professional standard," but by his achievement in making his character live, through his contribution to the full interpretation of the play.

When Laurence Olivier produced the film version of *Henry V* he did not approach his work as a professional, but as an artist. He brought to it all his experience and his knowledge. He applied these with imagination and invention. It was the combination of these faculties that made his work an outstanding success. It was not appraised because he was paid for doing it, but because it stimulated imagination and controlled thoughts and emotions. It was a work of art.

Can amateurs create works of art? Certainly. Many have done so. One has only to call to mind the work done by the Marlowe Society at Cambridge and the O.U.D.S. at Oxford to realize this truth; and there are numerous amateur societies that give performances of high merit. They do so because they are, first, aware of their function, and next because they set out sincerely to carry out that function.

One of the ways in which amateurs may assert their individual and independent natures is in their choice of play. They are bound to satisfy neither the egotism of an individual actor nor the cupidity of a financier.

They are free to choose where they will. By their choice they express their attitude towards their art, and, frequently, their estimate of their own abilities and tastes.

Mr. Sean O'Casey stated that it "was better for amateurs to do good plays badly than bad plays well." If amateurs had for their motto: "The play's the thing," they would never perform bad plays. There is no need for them to do so; and they should realize that they cannot hope to make such plays interesting. Good plays are interesting to both performers and audiences. A good play provides something worth remembering, something to talk about and discuss. It also provides the material from which the actor may deduce what he has to perform, and for this reason amateurs are likely to achieve greater success in good plays than they can hope to in poor plays.

Acting is at once an alluring pastime and an exciting experience. It provides a thrilling way of experiencing dramatic literature, and, at the same time, provides considerable fun for all taking part. Wherever one goes one finds groups of amateurs. Interest in acting has never been greater than it is to-day, and this has caused an enormous increase in the number of one-act plays. The many Drama Festivals and Competitions give to this form of play an added importance, but it must, unfortunately, be stated that far too many of these plays are very poor material for presentation. Worthless plays should be avoided. Their apparent simplicity should not be an excuse for selection.

Many amateur groups choose plays that have already been made popular on Broadway. There is nothing wrong in this provided the play is good, and provided there is no attempt to copy the Broadway production. Yet sometimes one wonders if the amateur is wise to place himself in direct competition and comparison with the professional. It is not suggested that the amateur should avoid all plays that are performed by professionals, for this would exclude the plays of Shakespeare, Shaw, and, indeed, many other good plays. What is suggested, is that all plays chosen should be interpreted from the plays themselves and studied and treated as if they were new plays.

As a change from one-act plays and well-known plays amateurs might consider giving performances of new plays, and those not well known. Such performances would provide interesting material for the actors and also for their friends. Plays by Pirandello, T. S. Eliot, Gordon Bottomley, W. B. Yeats, and many others should prove of considerable interest. Such ventures could prove exciting and worth while. Choice of play is almost unlimited for the amateur who is willing to experiment and acquire skill in speech and movement. The verse plays of T. S. Eliot and Christopher Fry provide excellent material and scope for those amateurs who have learnt to speak verse, and it is not beyond hope that such plays would be acceptable to the audiences which find pleasure in seeing friends perform. The less-performed plays of Shaw, such as *The Applecart* and *In Good King Charles's Golden Days*, would always be welcomed by audiences and would provide both interest and valuable experience for those rehearsing them.

Remember "The play's the thing." Choose boldly and well, so that when performance is over there remains a memory of something worth while.

CHAPTER VI

STYLE

ALL artists possess characteristics by which their work
may be recognized, and which establish them in
their particular field of expression.   While they inherit
from the past and accept much that is traditional, they
also use the freedom of the individual to express themselves in an original and personal way.

In their various ways, too, actors and actresses display
individual styles in their methods of acting.   In addition to a common technique, they have their own unique
way of presenting their chosen characters to an audience.

In the modern theatre there is considerable variety of
styles, even though the acting is rooted in a well-
established tradition.   Sir Laurence Olivier, Sir John
Gielgud, Michael Redgrave, and Donald Wolfit play
Lear, but each interpretation has the hall-mark of the
individual actor plainly engraved upon it.

Style, says the dictionary, "is the collective characteristics of artistic expression."   This bald definition
is hardly sufficient, however, to explain the power of
these artists.   In addition to characteristics that can be
enumerated, there is a quality which eludes description,
which lifts their work beyond the measure of technical
standards.   The style of Dame Edith Evans cannot
be explained by a list of characteristics.   In all her work
there is a quality that baffles and defies description, even
though it is familiar.   It is a personal quality that

transcends the technique which has been acquired by study and practice, something more than personality, even though personality is a part of it.

Style is that personal way of doing something which makes achievement unique and memorable.

Mannerisms and pretentiousness should not be confused with style. These are egotistical manifestations that declare self-importance, and bear little relation to the actor's problem of interpretation. Mannerisms may reveal the actor, but not the character he represents. Pretentiousness may make an appeal to the indiscriminate, but it cannot be a substitute for real ability.

A good style is, perhaps, the most elusive and difficult quality to pursue and capture. It demands integrity, sincerity, and the subordination of self. It rejects bombast, exaggeration, and meaningless gestures and postures. It imposes discipline and the utmost care in study and in performance alike. The essence of style is appropriateness. Speech, gesture, and deportment must be appropriate for the task in hand. There must be discretion in selection, and modesty in performance.

"O, it offends me to the soul to hear a robustious periwig-pated fellow tear a passion to tatters, to very rags, to split the ears of the groundlings ... Be not too tame neither, but let your own discretion be your tutor: suit the action to the word, the word to the action: with this special observance, that you o'er step not the modesty of nature: for any thing so overdone is from the purpose of playing, whose end, both at the first and now, was and is, to hold, as 'twere, the mirror up to nature; to show virtue her own feature, scorn her own image, and the very age and body of the time his form and pressure."

Hamlet's advice to the Players is still the best that can be given and followed.   Yet in it there may be detected a certain vagueness, for the actor's own discretion is to be his tutor.   Discretion carries a heavy burden, for it entails both knowledge and the power of making judgments.   Prudence and discernment must go with liberty of action, if discretion is to be wisely used.   Thus the burden of selection and the method of playing rests finally upon the actor himself, upon his own taste and judgment.   This is the aspect of acting that cannot be taught; it can be cultivated only from within the actor himself.   The actor's discrimination will determine all that he does, and will determine his style of acting.

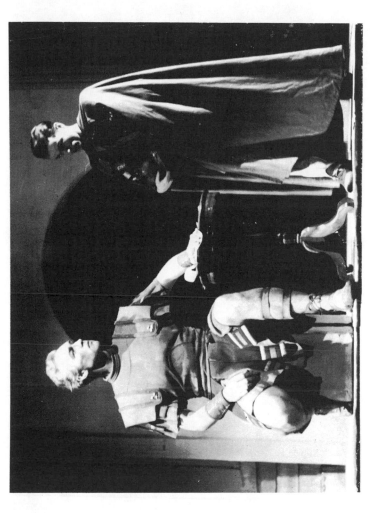

The Tent Scene from Shakespeare's "Julius Caesar," given at Hofstra College, N. Y.

Courtesy ANTA

"Twelfth Night" at the San Diego Shakespeare Festival, Old Globe Theatre, Balboa Park.

Courtesy ANTA

Sylvia Short, Geraldine Fitzgerald, Viveca Lindfors, and Orson Welles, appearing in the New York City Center production of Shakespeare's "King Lear," 1956.

Photo by Alix Jeffry, courtesy ANTA

Louis Calhern in the title role, as he appeared in the Broadway production of Shakespeare's "King Lear."

Photo by Vandamm, courtesy ANTA

Ernest Graves as Brutus, Roger Mandan as Anthony, Roger Starr as Lucius, James Glenn, Octavius Caesar, in the Shakespearewrights' presentation of "Julius Caesar."

Photo by Barbara and Justin Kerr, courtesy ANTA

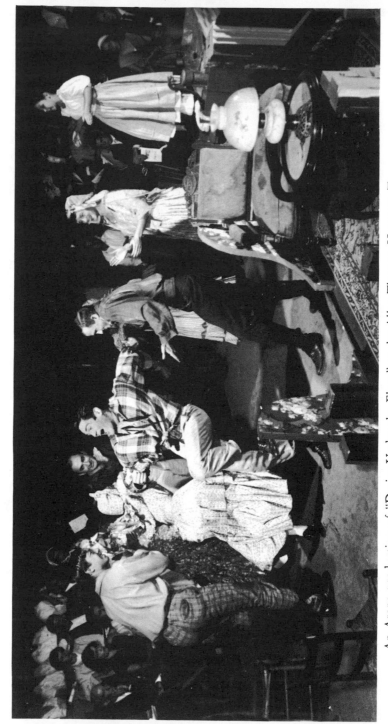

An Arena production of "Desire Under the Elms," at the Alley Theatre, Houston, Tex.

Courtesy ANTA

The Balcony Scene in "Romeo and Juliet," presented by the Kent State University.

Melvyn Blake as Friar John, Julie Harris as Juliet, Tony van Bridge as Friar Laurence, and Bruno Gerussi as Romeo, at the 1960 Stratford Shakespearean Festival, Ontario.

Photo by Roger Smith, courtesy ANTA

A scene from the Anta Playhouse production of "Desire Under the Elms" by Eugene O'Neill.

Photo by Vic Shifreen, courtesy ANTA

Christopher Hewett, Kenneth Mars, and Brewster Mason in a scene from "The Affair" by C. P. Snow; Henry Miller Theatre, 1962.

Photo by Werner J. Kuhn, courtesy ANTA

Another scene from the Broadway production of "The Affair," near end of Act I, shows Brewster Mason and Elizabeth Hubbard.

Photo by Werner J. Kuhn, courtesy ANTA

A scene from the Anta Theatre's New York production of "A Man For All Seasons," starring Paul Scofield, Leo McKern, George Rose, and Albert Dekker.

Courtesy ANTA

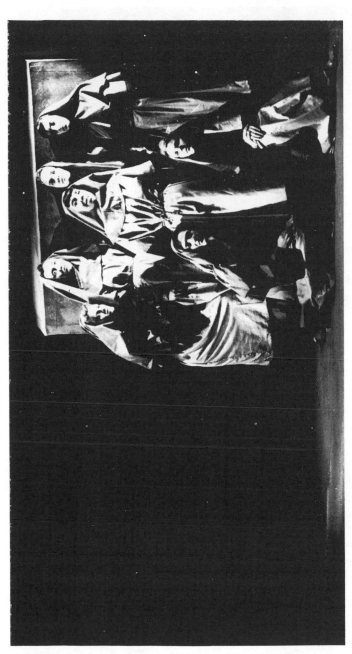

Eliot's "Murder in the Cathedral," as presented at the University Theatre of the University of Colorado.
Courtesy ANTA

The "92 Theatre" of Wesleyan University, Middletown, Conn., staged this production of "Murder in the Cathedral," the chorus is shown here.

Courtesy ANTA

A scene from Shakespeare's "Othello," as presented by the students of Ithaca College, N. Y.

Courtesy ANTA

Phyllis Thaxter and Art Carney in a scene from the Broadway production of "Take Her, She's Mine."

Photo by Fred Fehl, courtesy ANTA

Part II:
STAGE MOVEMENT

PREFACE

(Stage Movement)

by Margaret Leighton

PERFECT movement may not necessarily make a fine actor, but it must be one of the foremost tools in an actor's equipment, as must be a trained voice. Indisciplined movements and a harsh voice cannot kill the essential quality in an actor, but the development of these two can enhance that quality by giving it expression.

This book provides very good exercises that are intended to assist amateurs to attain professional standards. To study these and to adopt the suggestions that the author makes will be of real service to those who, attracted by the theatre, wish to become active workers in it.

INTRODUCTION

(*Stage Movement*)

MOVEMENT is expressive of personality whether it is made in social circles or in professional life.

This volume is principally concerned with Stage Movement, and has been written to help both students and players to move on the stage not only with ease and grace but also with the significance that characterization requires.

It is necessary for the player in order to portray character as conceived by the playwright to be artist and technician alike. When he or she is both, interpretation is sound and convincing. An actor or actress who moves clumsily or inartistically on the stage is noticed at once by the experienced playgoer.

The technique, or the mechanics, of movement can be mastered by the majority of students; technique linked with what is called "the artistic temperament" introduces psychological and other issues with which I do not deal in detail here. None the less, if the exercises provided are worked systematically and in conjunction with observance of the indications given on my Emotional Scale until facility is gained, progress towards the attainment of both skill and understanding will be made.

The exercises are designed to help students deliberately to create states of mind that are reflected in movement. These enable gradations of relaxation and tension, registered with the aid of the Emotional Scale, to be created and expressed through the art of acting.

The aim of subsequent chapters is to provide guidance and assistance to all who wish to become expert in the technique of stage movement and adept in characterization; but, basically, much depends upon the individual's aptitude, ability, determination, and perseverance. Without these the probability is that the assistance provided will not be exploited fully and skill and artistry will not be wholly achieved.

CHAPTER I

FEET WHEN SITTING, WALKING, AND STANDING

Sitting

THE technique of foot-work for a woman when sitting is different from that of a man. A man's movements are wider and away from the body and give a broadening effect, whereas a woman's are closer to the body and narrower. Economy of movement is essential for both.

Woman's Foot Movements.

Assume that a chair is level with a woman's L side. She walks to it until the back of her L leg touches the centre of the seat's edge. This ensures that she is near enough to sit comfortably but not on the chair's edge. She closes the R foot to the L foot, and lowers herself to the seat. If the chair is on her right, the technique is reversed and the seat is touched with the R leg. She should relax, not throw the body forward, but keep it upright as it is lowered to the seat.

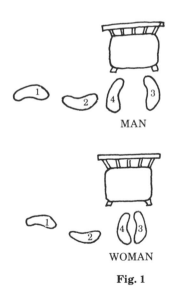

MAN

WOMAN

Fig. 1

The feet should be kept together, toe to toe, heel to heel. When she must turn to look behind, she should not step to the side and close, but keep the feet together and lift herself as she turns the trunk. This can be done without parting the feet. When crossing the knees, she should slide, not lift, one knee over the other. When uncrossing, she should slide again without lifting the knee, the down-coming foot closing immediately and tightly to the stationary foot.

Economy and the elimination of all unnecessary moves should be the aim.

Man's Sitting Technique. The same as woman's, but a man keeps his feet apart as he lowers himself to the chair (Fig. 1) immediately after touching the seat with

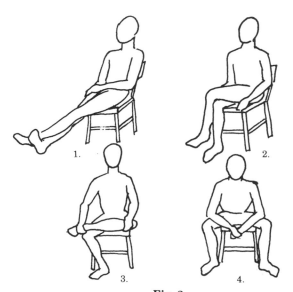

Fig. 2

the back of the L or R leg.   A man has a wider choice
of movement.   He may

(1) stretch his legs as he crosses them at the ankles;
(2) cross his knees;
(3) place one ankle over the knee of the other leg;
(4) have his feet wide apart.

These four positions are suggested (Fig. 2) as the basis
for sitting.   As co-ordination of the body is mastered, a
good sitting posture will develop naturally and unconsciously.   First, however, until confidence is gained,
a structure on which to work should be used.   A man
should move into a fresh position as he speaks and keep
still when he listens.

Rising—Woman's Technique.   Rise with the feet
together, more to the R with the R leg, or to the L
with the L leg.   Always use the limb nearer to where the
turn has to be made.

Walking

For walking the technique for man and woman is the
same.

Walk with the feet straight, not turned in or out.
Practise walking on an imaginary straight line, the feet
just brushing each other in passing, the heel leading; the
movement of the leg comes from the hip, not the knees.
This keeps a central balance (Fig. 3).

RIGHT
Fig. 3

If two lines are used, a swaying or rolling movement occurs as the balance is transferred from the R to the L

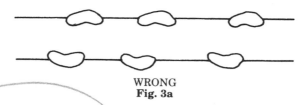

WRONG
Fig. 3a

foot.   Carry the weight of the body on the balls of the feet; do not drop on the heels; keep the weight forward.

Standing

Woman's Technique.   Never stand with the feet apart. When coming to a standstill, bring the back foot to the stationary foot, and touch it.   Keep the weight on the front stationary foot.   Relax the knee of the back leg drawn up to touch the stationary foot (Fig 4).

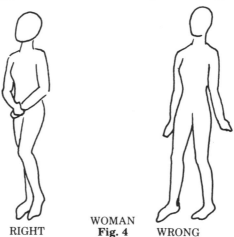

RIGHT   WOMAN   WRONG
Fig. 4

Man's Standing Movement. When coming to a standstill, bring the back foot nearly level—not close—to the stationary foot, and keep the weight on the foot in front (Fig. 5, Woman).

In the standing position, the woman's feet touch and the man's do not. The principle is breadth and apartness away from the body (man's movements) and together and to the body (woman's movements).

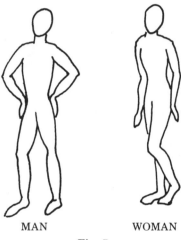

MAN   WOMAN

Fig. 5

CHAPTER II

HANDS WHEN SITTING, STANDING, AND WALKING

SELF-CONSCIOUSNESS often manifests itself through the hands. These should be controlled and kept still so that when a gesture is used it is significant. Nervous movements divide and diminish power. Unless a man or woman knows what to do with the hands when he or she has to sit, difficulties arise.

Hands on Sitting. Woman's Position

As the body is lowered to a seat and the feet are closed, the hands should be clasped, with the elbows touching the body, waist level—these movements being

 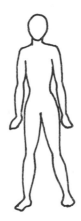

RIGHT   WRONG

WOMAN
Fig. 6

done simultaneously as the feet are closed. The hands should be relaxed (still clasped) into the lap as she sits, and remain there until the sitting position is changed.

Never move the hand indefinitely. Know where you are going to put it and why. Keep it STILL until another body movement has to be made. Co-ordinate

The woman, on rising, may clasp
her hands at waist level, and release them
as she walks away.
Fig. 7

the hand movement *with* these other movements simultaneously. Co-ordination keeps the body a complete unit or whole, does not break attention, and creates repose and economy of movement.

The man, on rising, may put his hands
in his pockets.
Fig. 8

Always aim at economy. For example, do not use a hand movement to indicate a chair on the line "Won't you sit down?" Eliminate all unnecessary movement,

On rising, keep the body upright.
Fig. 9

and keep the hands still until they have to be moved for a definite purpose.

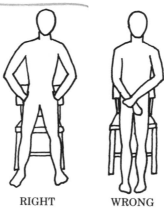

RIGHT   WRONG
MAN
Fig. 10

Hands when Standing—Woman

The positions and mechanics are similar to those for sitting. Do not fidget. Keep the hands still when they are not being moved for a specific purpose, i.e. to take a book, to answer the telephone, to shake hands, to light a cigarette. When coming to a standstill, clasp the hands waist level with the elbows in, as the feet come together simultaneously. To leave the hands at the sides is not wrong, but there they are more difficult to keep still. When walking release them to the sides.

Hands when Walking

As the arms swing slightly backwards and forwards, the hands should almost brush the hips with the palms. They should be in alignment with the body, not swing across the front of it. The hands and fingers should be relaxed, unless there is mental tension. Avoid "toast rack" fingers by keeping the first three fingers together (Fig. 11).

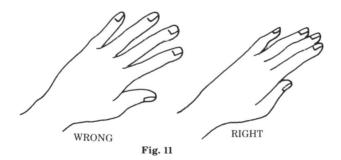

WRONG   RIGHT

Fig. 11

The technique is similar for men, with the exception that the hands should not be brought together and clasped when sitting. The elbows need not touch the sides. When a man is sitting, the hands should be controlled. Give them something to do, i.e. lift a trouser

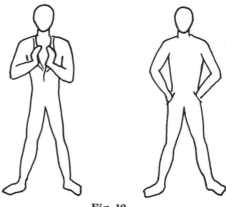

Fig. 12

crease or put them into the pockets, or, when standing, place them in the pockets or hold a lapel (Fig. 12).

Fig. 13

The back of the knuckles may be placed on the hip, not the palm, as with women (Fig. 13).

In this chapter I have in mind the hands of a poised, controlled player, not one who is nervous, tired, bored, or angry. Nervousness shows immediately in the hands. With these, as with the feet, it is essential to know where to place them and when to keep them still, until a movement is made *on speech* into another position. For two reasons they should not be moved when a player is listening:

(1) When attention is arrested the body is also arrested, the mind holding it still;

(2) movement on another player's speech divides the audience's interest, often through a player's inattention to what another player is saying.

A player, when shaking hands, gives the right hand to the other player, who takes it with a firm grasp. This is enough. A pump-handle effect is created if the hand is shaken up and down. Aim at economy of movement.

CHAPTER III

THE ARMS—CO-ORDINATION AND OPPOSITION

ARM movement should be from the shoulder, and not stop at the elbow (Fig. 14). The scapula should move freely. Then the object of the gesture—the shaking of hands, the raising of a hat, the putting on of a glove, cap, or cloak, waving good-bye, giving a welcome—will be communicated. A single gesture, without dialogue, can speak volumes. Practise this movement in front of a mirror and note how restricted it is at first. It will seem to come mostly from the elbow. The hand belongs to the arm, and as the arm expresses itself, the hand must continue the expression to the tips of the fingers. There is no welcome expressed by the arms, if the hands are limp and lifeless. Do not confuse arm movements that include the hands with hand movements that do not involve the whole arm, as in eating, knitting, or writing.

Decide that a movement is primarily an arm or a hand movement, and apply the appropriate technique.

Co-ordinate arm and leg movements. For example, as you step forward to shake hands, move the leg and arm together; do not step and raise the arm afterwards.

Stand sideways before a large mirror. Draw on a pair of long-elbow gloves, actual or imaginary, and move the whole arm from the shoulder. Repeat, but move the arm from the elbow only—the natural inclination.   This movement is inhibited.   To put on a pair of gloves is a movement that produces quality and style.   Do it slowly.

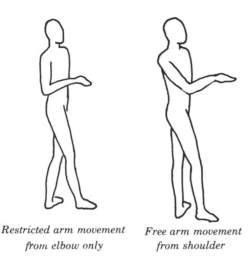

Restricted arm movement   *Free arm movement*
from elbow only   *from shoulder*

Fig. 14

Practise raising your hat or using a walking stick, by moving the entire arm freely from the shoulder.   Each time note and check the two ways and their differences.

CHAPTER IV

THE EYES

EYES can make or mar a player's performance. When they are focused on an object they have life and meaning and direct attention to the point of concentration.

Perfect control acquired by mastery of the essential mechanics achieves a finished and moving performance.

When playing to another player look at his EYES, not at his nose, ears, mouth, tie, or buttonhole. This will give him the sense of being spoken to. If he gives you similar attention, his eyes on yours, communication will flow between you and hold not only each other's attention but also that of the audience.

To develop control of the eyes, enter a room and make an announcement to a sitting person who must concentrate her attention on your eyes as you talk to her eyes. Will-power must be exerted deliberately. Repeat in the presence of a third person, neither player concentrating on the other's eyes. This will demonstrate that the first way is the better.

Link with this exercise control of the hands. Ask a member of the audience to note if the hands are still. They should not be nervous or fidgety. Obviously, the mechanics of stage movement must be known before a finished performance can be given.

CHAPTER V

THE HEAD

THE carriage of the head, the heaviest part of the body, if correct, gives superb strength and dignity. Lengthen the neck, keep the shoulders down, lift the head, keep the chin in, and the EYES LEVEL. Much depends on the eyes. Downcast eyes make the head droop; lifted eyes take the head up. Dancers in training keep their eyes on one of the hands and follow it as it circles and falls, etc., in order to encourage head movement.

Place the feet together, with the R arm stretched out horizontally and at right angles to the body. Keep the eyes on a given point, say, on the index finger of the R hand. Swing the R arm in front of the body, over to the L, above the head, and drop it to the side. Next swing it backwards and forwards, and to the side once more. During these eight moves the eyes must never leave the index finger.

Keep the head still and poised when attention is focused on a stationary object. Nods and bobs divide the power to express emotion. Meaning should be expressed by the tension of the whole body.

Walk round the room with a book on your head to develop a good head carriage. Lengthen the neck and pull the shoulders down. Walk without the book, and note the difference. Watch each other, criticize and correct.

In a scene tell excitedly of something that has happened, and keep the head still. This must not be confused with turning it when the eyes are focused on a given object. The movement directs and fixes the attention, but does not divide it.

CHAPTER VI

WALKING

S TAND still, with the feet together, and check that
 the posture is correct. Make sure you are not
sagging. Pull back the knees, pull in the abdominal
muscles, lift the diaphragm, expand the chest, pull back
the shoulders, lift the head, and lengthen the neck to
help to pull down the shoulders. The general feeling
of the whole body, with the exception of the shoulders,
is of uplift, of being pulled away from gravitation. The
shoulders should be consciously pulled down continuously (Fig. 15).

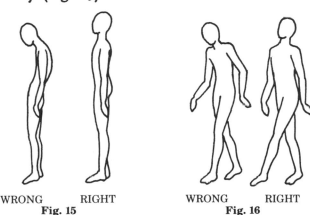

WRONG   RIGHT   WRONG   RIGHT
Fig. 15   **Fig. 16**

Do not keep tense; as you walk, the movement must
be fluid. Start to walk as one unit from the hips, not
from the knees, taking the weight of the body forward

with each step (Fig. 16). Think of the hips as the carrier of the trunk, with the movement coming from them, and keep the trunk and head steady. Swing the leg forward from the hips, take a long step, and use an imaginary line on which to place the feet as described in Chapter I. The arms should be relaxed and swing with the impetus of the walking movement in opposition to the moving leg, i.e. the L arm forward to the R leg and vice versa. Similarly, there should be a slight opposition movement between the hips and the forward-moving leg. This is exaggerated in the walk of a mannequin. With lack of opposition of hips and leg, for example, the R hip and the R leg moving forward together, a gauche, awkward walk develops.

Keep in mind these points, and practise walking continuously. After walking, when coming to a standstill, bring the back foot up so that it touches the front standing foot (Fig· 17). The back knee should be relaxed and the weight on the front foot. Never end with feet apart. A man may bring the back foot level with, but not closed to, the standing foot.

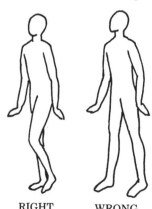

RIGHT   WRONG
Walking to a standstill
Fig. 17

PRACTICE AT
REHEARSAL
TURN INTO EXERCISE —
INCLUDING MAKING EYE
CONTACT

CHAPTER VII

BODY MOVEMENT

IMAGINE the top half of the body and the lower half—below the hips—as a pair of scales that remain perfectly balanced by *opposition of movement*. For example, if the R leg has stepped forward, the L hip and the L shoulder are forward, and vice versa, to balance this movement. Stepping forward without this opposition of movement, with the L leg, L hip, and L shoulder forward, you would fall to the L because the action would be from one side, particularly when bending or stooping. Scales must be evenly weighted in order to be balanced. The Greeks based their dancing and physical culture on the principle of opposition of movement. To apply this, practise standing with the feet together. Stepping forward on the R foot, simultaneously swing the opposite hip and shoulder forward, keeping the head level and the eyes forward (Fig. 18). Step back with the R foot, closing the feet and straightening the hip and shoulders. Repeat with the L foot, this time going into a knee-bending position, as though to pick something from the ground. The R hip and the R shoulder forward will maintain the balance, and the R hand, being in opposition to the L foot, will pick up the object. (Fig. 19)

The hand that comes forward belongs to the shoulder that is forward in opposition to the foot. It is not

Julie Haydon appeared in this performance of Shakespeare's "Twelfth Night" at Millikin University, Decatur, Ill.

The Tybalt-Mercutio Duel Scene from "Romeo and Juliet," as given by the Dartmouth Players, Dartmouth College, Hanover, N. H.

Courtesy ANTA

enough for the hand alone to make the opposition; it must come from the shoulders.

Fig. 18

Practise these exercises with a companion. Cross to each other, say "How do you do?" and shake hands as you step forward with the L foot, with the R hip and shoulder forward, and the R hand extended.

Practise many times until opposition of movement is co-ordinated.

Walk up to an object on the ground, pick it up with the opposition of movement, walk up to your companion, and give him it in opposition.

Fig. 19

Walk to a standstill, and close up the back foot, checking that hips and shoulders are in opposition to the front foot. This will assist poise and assurance when you stand still. Any movement that involves taking up an object is done with opposition of movement.

When sitting, do not bring your R shoulder forward if your R knee is crossed. *Bring forward* the shoulder

Fig. 20

opposite to the crossed knee, *which comes forward.* As the hand belonging to the back shoulder demands rest, put it on the hip or the back of a chair, or in a pocket, making sure that the arm moves back (Fig. 20).

For example, do not put the R hand on the hip if the R shoulder is forward. A backward movement is necessary, so use the hand of the backward shoulder.

Practise the following sitting positions until opposition is mastered, and correct the feet, if they are apart.

Sit with the feet together and with the hands clasped in the lap. Cross the R knee over the L knee, and, simultaneously, bring the L shoulder forward with the L hand on the knee, taking the R hand back on the R hip. Repeat this, crossing the L knee over the R knee and reversing the opposition of the shoulders, arms, and hands. See that the feet close together immediately during the uncrossing and recrossing of the knees (Fig. 21).

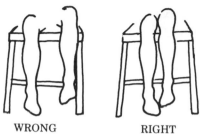

WRONG   RIGHT

Fig. 21

Turning on a Stage-cross

If you have to cross in order to sit in a chair down stage, turn upstage as you reach the chair with your back to the proscenium arch. This will help you to keep your attention on the stage. Also think of being in your

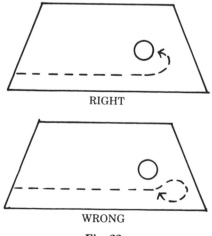

RIGHT

WRONG

Fig. 22

own four-walled sitting-room. With the interest in, not outside, the room, you would naturally turn your attention to the room, not the wall. On the stage you do not talk to the audience, but to the players; therefore think of the proscenium arch as the fourth wall of your room.

Always turn towards the shoulder nearer your object. Often a player turns away and faces downstage before he reaches and faces his objective (Fig. 22).

This is almost impossible to believe, but try it.

If you are alone on the stage and have to cross to take a book from a shelf and re-cross to your chair, use stage centre as your turning point. Which shoulder is nearer the centre? Turn towards that shoulder.

You have to approach another player who is walking; turn in the direction of the shoulder that is nearer to him. Do not be afraid to turn your back to the audience. It is unnecessary to fully face the audience in order to make the voice carry: a sideways attitude enables the voice to be heard.

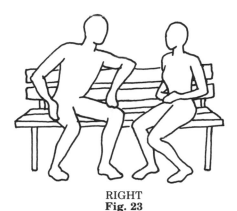

RIGHT
Fig. 23

When talking to another player, turn the whole body, including the feet, towards him. It is irritating to

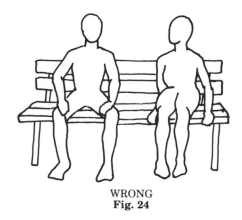

WRONG
Fig. 24

watch two players on a sofa, with their shoulders, hips, and feet facing the audience, only occasionally turning the head in the other's direction (Figs. 23 & 24).

Avoid standing in front of or directly behind another actor.
Fig. 25

Each should be given full attention. The body of
the one should be turned in the direction of the other,
and news of one should reflect the spirit of the text so
that it can be reflected by the other.

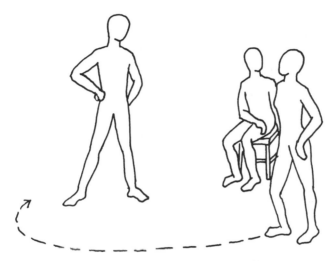

Avoid talking directly upstage. Walk
level to the player to whom you are speaking.
Fig. 26

Be quite sure of the ground design : moves and stage
directions are easily memorized. The producer may
direct a move down-stage R, i.e. that would be the
player's right and the producer's L as he faces him.

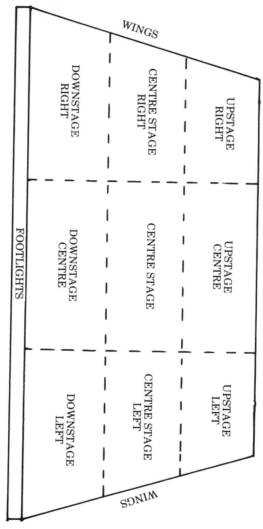

WINGS

DOWNSTAGE RIGHT

CENTRE STAGE RIGHT

UPSTAGE RIGHT

FOOTLIGHTS

DOWNSTAGE CENTRE

CENTRE STAGE

UPSTAGE CENTRE

DOWNSTAGE LEFT

CENTRE STAGE LEFT

UPSTAGE LEFT

WINGS

Fig. 27

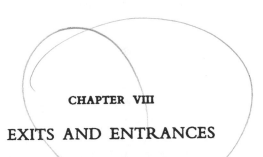

CHAPTER VIII

EXITS AND ENTRANCES

A N entrance, paradoxically, must be seen, and yet
not seen. The audience's attention must be caught
at once and held by the player's entrance. The
mechanics of opening and closing a door must be

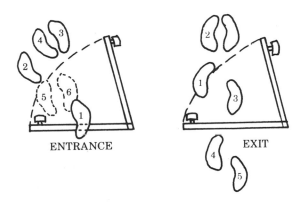

ENTRANCE   EXIT

Fig. 28

controlled so that the player's attention is on a specific object on the stage, and not on the door.

If on an entrance a character has to be greeted, attention must be concentrated on the character. A glance back at the door would show that it was uppermost in mind and that attention was divided.

Know what you are about, and then forget the mechanics. Enter a room with the question: "Why have I entered this room?"

Here is an exercise on making an entrance when the door is closed.

Assume that the handle is on the left of the door. Take hold of it with the R hand. As you push the door open, starting with the R foot, take three steps forward. On the third step pass the door and grasp the inner side of the door handle with your L hand, closing the L foot to the R foot. This makes the fourth step and prevents standing with the feet apart. Now with the L hand close the door, step to it with the L foot, and close the R foot to the L foot—fifth and sixth steps.

Exits. Assume that the door handle is on the R. Step to it on the R foot, and grasp it with the L hand. As you pull it towards you, step back with the R foot, closing it to the L foot, the door passing to your L side. Step forward with the L foot and close the door with the R hand. Grasp the handle on the under, not on the top, side, otherwise the R shoulder will be hunched. It should be down as you pull the door behind to close it.

Practise this until you can speak your line satisfactorily while making your exit and still be in full control of the door. Players, when practising an exit, often make a complete circle on closing the door and end by walking out backwards!

Do not fidget once you have made an entrance. Walk directly to your position, or, if you have to stand, enter with poise and maintain it. Now you should know what to do with your feet, hands, head, eyes, and body.

CHAPTER IX

MECHANICS OF THE EMOTIONAL RANGE

THE physical effect of the emotional range shows itself in complete relaxation to absolute tension. Use a scale of 1 to 10, base the relaxation of a man in a faint on 1 and the tension of a man stiff with fear on 10.

A player must be able to relax physically. The first exercise begins with complete relaxation at 1 on the scale.

Stand with the feet slightly apart, the knees relaxed, the weight rather forward on the balls of the feet, the abdominal muscles, diaphragm, and shoulder girdle relaxed (the two arms dangling over the feet) and the head down, as in Fig. 29. Relax the facial muscles and mouth, let the eyes close; relax, relax, relax, 1, begin to uncurl slightly; 2, uncurl further, though the head and the back of the neck are still relaxed; 3, still uncurl so that you are almost upright; 4, 5, lift the head and take the shoulders (scapula) back. Now you are in an upright position (Fig. 30). Under 5 on the Emotional Scale is relaxation in varying degrees and over 5 mounting degrees of tension; 6, raise the arms slightly; 7, raise the arms higher, with slight tension throughout the body; 8, lift the arms shoulder level, with tension growing and to the tips of fingers; 9, lift the arms up to V with tension still growing; 10, stretch the arms with high tension held throughout the whole body and limbs—keep the heels down for control (Fig. 31).

126

Now to relax to 1.

Repeat the whole exercise until you can completely relax at 1.

Breathe in from 1–10.   Breathe out from 10–1.

With practice, you will know when you are tense and when you are not quite relaxed.

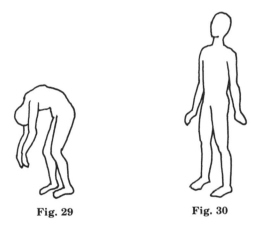

Fig. 29   Fig. 30

On mounting from 1–10 do not by-pass *any* of the scale; for example, 1, 3, 4, 7, 10.   All the grades must be passed through, felt, and realized.   On 10 coming to 1, collapse completely and quickly.   Imagine on 10 that your arms are strung up by a rope, that it is cut suddenly, and that you collapse.

A common fault at the beginning is to keep the tension in the elbows and wrists on the change from 10 to 1.   These will be the first to crumple with the head and shoulder girdle.   On reaching 1 the arms should be dangling and waving slightly with the impetus.   If they

are *still*, there is rigidity somewhere.   Do not *put* your-
self-down: flop.

If a player has to convey the extreme tension of fear
and his little finger is relaxed, he will not be wholly
convincing.   Therefore, when at 10 make certain that
tension is at the tip of each finger.   Similarly, at 1 there
must be complete relaxation.

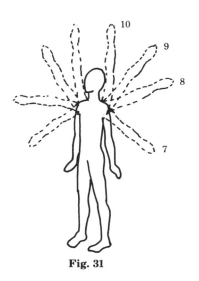

Fig. 31

When a player has to faint from a standing position,
no harm is done to the body if as it falls it is relaxed
absolutely.

When this 1–10 Emotional Scale of Relaxation to
Tension and Tension to Relaxation is practised and
mastered, try on reaching 1 from 10, to fall.   The ease
with which this can be done may surprise.   Indeed, if

relaxation has been mastered completely, to remain on the feet after coming from 10 to 1 will be difficult.   The natural inclination is to sink to the floor!   No rising of tension even to 2 must occur at this stage.

When the mechanics of this exercise are thoroughly understood and controlled, much has been achieved. Be at ease in your mind, undisturbed by props too near, as tension and relaxation are influenced by thoughts.

Some corresponding feelings on the 1–10 Emotional Scale :

Fear	.	.	. 10	Absolute Tension
Anger	.	.	. 9	
Resentment	.		. 8	
Apprehension	.		. 7	
Surprise	.	.	. 6	Tension grows
Poised	.	.	. 5	——————————
Disappointment	.		. 4	Tension diminishes
Fatigue	.	.	. 3	
Shock	.	.	. 2	
Faint	.	.	. 1	Complete Relaxation

Two drama students from Stanford and the University of
Washington, respectively, are shown in the Death Bed Scene
from the Oregon Shakespearean Festival's production of
"Othello."

Carol Stone and Karl Malden in the Broadway production of
O'Neill's "Desire Under The Elms."
Photo by Halley Erskine, courtesy ANTA

CHAPTER **X**

THE MECHANICS OF RELAXATION AND TENSION

SIT on a chair and try this exercise for two minutes. At first it will seem long. Ask someone to time it and to call out the quarter minutes. This is helpful. It allows full concentration on the exercise and develops timing for dramatic pause.

Tense up to 10 and hold the tension until you are sure every member of the body is tensed to the maximum. Then you will be ready to begin.

Without moving externally, come down the range, passing through 9 8 7 6 5 4 3 2 1 in two minutes. All the muscles should now be completely relaxed.

Although no external movement has taken place, the internal movement and change have been considerable. True relaxation comes from inside, not by merely holding oneself in a relaxed-looking position and moving in what may be thought is a relaxed way. One *is* or *is not* completely relaxed.

When the mechanics of this exercise have been mastered, the player will realize the varying degrees of his emotional range and capacity, and his acting, mentally, physically, and vocally, will become more vivid. Instead of playing a limited range between 4 and 6, he will develop his full capacity between 1–10.

Most players find it easier to play above than below

5, the reason being that daily existence keys the scale high because of mental conflicts and concentrations that produce, in turn, tensions in the body.

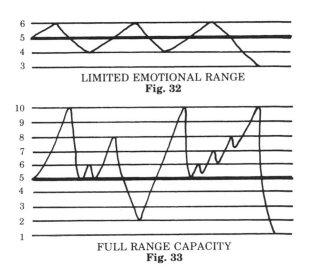

LIMITED EMOTIONAL RANGE
Fig. 32

FULL RANGE CAPACITY
Fig. 33

When practising relaxation empty the mind of thoughts as you get lower down the scale. Do not be anxious; anxiety tenses. To learn to relax is difficult, but the aim can be achieved with practice and patience. Begin to check on your own emotional scale during daily life.

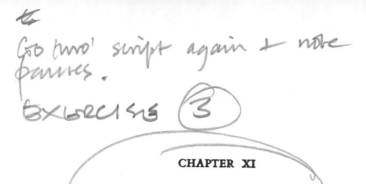

CHAPTER XI

THE MECHANICS OF PAUSE

DO not be afraid to pause. At the moment that physical outward movement is arrested, you will most powerfully command attention. Concentrated attention is magnetic. When a player is told something of great importance, he will respond, either going up to Tension or down to Relaxation, but he will not move externally; internally he will (see Chapter X). When he moves he ends (breaks) the dramatic pause. His first move tells his reaction to the news.

At the beginning of the pause on, say, the line "You have won the high jump", he will mount to 10 on the scale, starting from, say, 4, if he is seated. As he takes in the significance of the news he will mount, without moving externally, the scale 4, 5, 6, 7, 8, 9, 10, to complete the inner tension, which his movement, as he breaks the pause, betrays. So, too, does his voice. Do not go beyond 10, otherwise you will be out of control, physically and mentally. Your voice will squeak, and you will overplay.

A player on being given news that relaxes during the dramatic pause, applies the mechanics similarly but descends the scale. On, say, the line "There is no hope" and during the pause when he registers this fact he will come down to 1 and faint. If he comes down to 2, he will be just capable of movement and speech.

An expert dramatist sees that a player at the beginning

of the dramatic pause is at, say, 9 before bringing him down to 1, and vice versa before going up to 10 during the dramatic pause.

Lennox Robinson's *Crabbed Youth and Age* gives a simple example. Mrs. Swan, who is ill, is resting on the sofa. The scene is subdued. Only one lamp is lit. Six young people, on the floor and a sofa, are listening to a poem about moonlight. At 3 on the scale Mrs. Swan jumps up and cries, "Stop! I want lights, music, and dancing." Here is the dramatic pause, during which the tension rises from 3 to 10, on which the players jump to their feet. "Mrs. Swan!" "Mother!" "You will knock yourself up." Music and dancing follow.

Had this scene started at 5 instead of 3, and after the pause movement occurred at 7 instead of 10, the vivid dramatic element would not have been created. Do not be afraid of a long pause. Concentrated attention is a magnetic quality. Look at the eyes of the teller who has given you the news, and the audience will look at you. For example, a woman baking a cake casts the same spell on the watcher; she is concentrating and is completely unselfconscious and in being so frees her personality.

If there are several players on the stage during the dramatic pause, no move should be made until it is broken deliberately by speech by the player to whom the news has been given. If a player moves, attention will be transferred from the central character to the mover, and both the pause and the scene will be ruined.

Movement distracts. Keep still when listening so that the audience's attention is not divided. When a player watches with interest, the tension of the body indicates it. When interest is not shown, the player's attitude is indicated clearly to the audience. Movement comes from the mind—the cause. The effect is shown through the body.

CHAPTER XII

THE EMOTIONAL RANGE—MENTAL AND VOCAL

THE mechanics of the method of the 1–10 Emotional Scale explained in Chapter IX should have helped the player to control the varying degrees of tensions of his body. Now, how thoughts affect it, and how a character behaves in given circumstances, should be studied.

Questions the player should ask himself are: What will this character think during this entrance? Will his thoughts disturb him or will he be tranquil? A great deal depends upon the player's ability to return the correct answers. Remember, the varying degrees of tension come from the mind; the results show through the body.

Thoughts that create anger, hatred, jealousy, envy, fear, excitement, are fairly easy to recognize as being high on the Emotional Scale. The lower tensions must not be over-played. For example, if a character feels surprise and plays it at 9 on the scale instead of 7, it will distort by its dramatic content and cause confusion. If the dramatic content is not understood by the player, the dramatist's intention is not communicated in interpretation.

When the mind is empty, this state is also low on the Scale. Again, the half-tones, such as disappointment and sorrow, are more difficult to recognize. The player should ask himself whether he has accepted, say, disappointment, or whether he is fighting it. If he is, he will know that his Emotional Scale is above 5; how much above depends on the degree and intensity of his thoughts. Characters with nervous or phlegmatic temperaments are easily understood. The player needs to know the character's category. The reactions of the character with a nervous temperament are different from that of the phlegmatic character. To understand these points helps sound characterization.

The voice also reflects height or depth on the Emotional Scale. During high tension the breathing becomes shallow, is upper costal, and above the axilla—armpit. This produces a high tone that is shrill when the player reaches 10 on the Emotional Scale. Care should be taken not to go beyond. When the player is below 5 on the Scale, the breathing becomes deep lower costal (below the axilla). This produces lower vocal tones that are in character with the degrees of relaxation in movement.

CHAPTER XIII

CHARACTERIZATION OF FEET IN YOUTH, MIDDLE AGE, AND OLD AGE

Youth

UP to, say, fourteen years of age, the feet and knees tend to turn inwards. In characterization of move- ment, all "straight" technique is altered in accordance

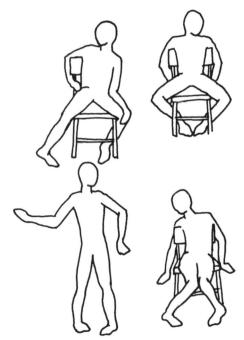

Fig. 34

with the character portrayed. For example, the feet are not closed on sitting, and the knees are not necessarily kept closed. The player asks himself what he would do

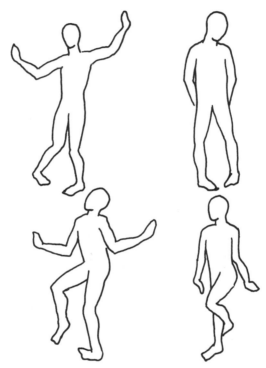

Fig. 35

with his limbs in certain circumstances. Follow the main structure given here and build upon it (Fig 34).

Youth, when sitting, has the toes and knees tending inwards, the feet being slightly apart and the movements quick. The feet are kicked out or twined round the leg of a chair, preferably with an inward movement. The legs are sprawled and stretched, often with the heels down and the toes up, movement from one position to another being restless. Movement in general is wide and away from the body; the pace quick, jerky, staccato, and lacking in economy, with restlessness a characteristic.

Standing. Similar characteristics to those when sitting are shown by youth, the toes and the knees being inclined inwards. The feet are not held together, but tend to feel the ground, drawing a circle with the toe, standing on one leg, using a hop, skip, and jump from time to time. The pace is quick, the general tension in movement being at 7 on the Emotional Scale (Fig. 35).

Walking. Two lines (indicated in Chapter I) are often used, though one line for central balance emerges from time to time. Again, the toes and the knees tend

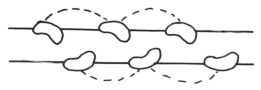

Fig. 36

to turn inwards. The heels are put down first, with the toes uplifted more than they are by mature adults. A circular swinging movement from the hip repeatedly occurs as the feet are put down and with one leg more than the other. Hops, skips, and jumps interrupt the walk from time to time (Fig. 36).

Middle Age

The Feet. For characters from seventeen to forty years of age mostly straight technique can be applied

(see Chapter I). The balance is central, and only one
line is, or should be, used in poised movement.

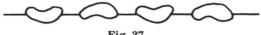

Fig. 37

Straight. On sitting, the feet and the knees are
together (Chapter I). The main difference in the
characterization of a girl of seventeen and of a woman of
forty is in pace; the girl has quick, spontaneous movements; the woman, deliberate, slow movements, with
greater economy.

Standing. The feet and knees are together on getting
up. After coming to a standstill, the back leg is moved
up to the front foot and closed, leaving no space. The

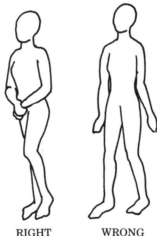

RIGHT   WRONG
Fig. 38

weight is rather more on the ball of the front foot, and
the knee of the back leg is relaxed. Care should be
taken not to have the feet apart when standing (Fig. 38).

Walking. The feet are straight and brush each other as they are moved. The weight of the body is carried over the forward-moving leg. Care should be taken

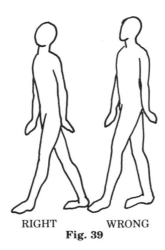

RIGHT   WRONG
Fig. 39

not to let the weight drop backwards on to the back foot. As the front foot moves forward, take the weight with it. Swing the entire leg from the hips (Fig. 39).

Old Age

The feet and the knees in old age turn outwards. Two lines are used, keeping the feet apart. The pace is slow.

Sitting. Little movement occurs. The legs are rarely crossed and then by men only. Women keep the knees apart; men tend to keep them together (Fig. 40). Feet of both men and women turn outwards and are placed flatly on the ground. The knee joints are rigid and give trouble on any bending movement. Movement is from the knee, not the hips, and increasingly so

with advancing age.   In general, from the age of forty
years the feet begin to turn outwards, and this is
particularly apparent when standing.

The feet are no longer together when men or women
sit.   They remain apart.

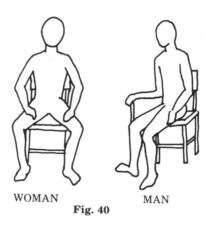

WOMAN   MAN
Fig. 40

On lowering the body to a seat, the trunk is thrown
forward.   The joints are stiff, and there is no relaxation.
When the body is raised to a standing position, the trunk
is again thrown forward, and much tension, say 8 on the
scale, is felt.   The pace is very slow throughout.   The
greater the age, the slower the movement.

CHAPTER XIV

HANDS OF YOUTH, MIDDLE AGE, AND OLD AGE

Youth

IN youth the fingers tend to spread and the hand has a squarer appearance than during any other period. It appears to be part of the wrist; there is not much turn or droop; this comes later.

Sitting. As the body is lowered to a seat, either the hands should grasp an object or the arms wave carelessly in order to maintain balance. The hands are uncontrolled and restless, and they move quickly. As youth sits, the hands point at an object, rub the eyes, push the hair out of the eyes, find something to do.

Fig. 41

Standing. The hands are either clasped behind the back or hung loosely at the sides when they are not in motion. Movement is similar to that described in sitting.

The hands often grasp an object, the fingers being spread round the object, with the palms flat and touching it (Fig. 41).

Walking. The hands tend to swing away from the body and do not brush the sides. They are alive to the finger tips and in constant movement.

Middle Age

When a player is mature, the hands indicate clearly the kind of character portrayed. The degree at which they

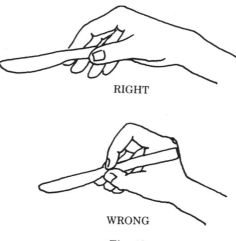

RIGHT

WRONG

Fig. 42

are tensed or relaxed expresses emotional feelings. How the fingers touch or pick up objects and how the wrist is curved as these movements are made are shown.

Characteristics of the intelligent, cultured, and sophisticated are slowness and, especially, economy of movement. A circular turn from the wrist is apparent, with much flexibility and a drooping wrist.

The fingers are not widespread, but are kept together, with the thumbs in. To keep the index and second fingers together is helpful. For an exercise eat and drink at a table, using a spoon, a knife and fork, and a tumbler or wine glass. Keep the pace slow (Fig. 42).

A navvy moves quickly and uses hands for emphasis, the pace being quick and jerky.

When a player is studying a part, the occupation and costume of the character to be portrayed should be noted in detail in order to find out the characteristics of the movements of the hands. Actually, they are influenced by the necessities of daily life. For example, a barrister may hold his lapel because of his habit of holding his robe in court, or cup his chin as he thinks out a problem, or put his hands on his hips from his habit of pushing back his robes. There is a reason for characteristic gesture; the player's responsibility when building a character is to find it.

A player's emotion is betrayed by his hands (Chapter X). To reach $9\frac{1}{2}$ on the Emotional Scale and to leave the fingers relaxed will not suffice: the hands, whether they are highly tensed or absolutely relaxed, must portray the full emotion. Therefore, discover what the hands should do and the varying degrees that must be registered on the 1–10 Emotional Scale.

Old Age

The hands tend to lose flexibility of wrist movement, become stiff, rigid, and bent, and the fingers incline to spread. A partial return is made to the one-piece movement of youth, but the hands move slowly, deliberately, and fumble. These characteristics are accentuated with advancing age.   How a player takes his spectacles from his pocket and out of their case, eventually resting them on his nose and placing the hooks of the frame behind his ears, calls for concentration and tells much about the age of the character: the pace of the hands, fingering, the immobility of the joints of the fingers, and the stiff immobile wrist—all are revealing.   Make-up can help, but must not be depended on.   The hands by their movements tell their age.

CHAPTER XV

ARMS OF YOUTH, MIDDLE AGE, AND OLD AGE

Youth

THE arms are free and uninhibited; the movement comes from the scapula and is unrestricted. They swing and gesticulate constantly. When youth is seated, eating, drinking, or sewing, the elbows tend to be outwards from, not into, the body. The arms are swung shoulder level and above the head, then turn out

Fig. 43

and away from the body. Sometimes they are swung behind the back with the hands clasped. When putting on a garment, it will often be flung over the head with the arms raised in order to place them into the sleeves instead of moving them downwards in order to reach the armhole. When youth is seated, the arms do not come to the sides, but tend to be thrown outwards and to dangle at the sides (Fig. 45). Elbows are away from the body or the arms raised, the movement coming directly from the scapula, and not from the elbow only.

Fig. 44

This applies to walking, during which much swinging and movement of the arms occur. There is a gradual lessening during adolescence, when the general movement is inhibited and awkward.

Middle Age

During the period from, say, eighteen to forty, there are variations mainly in the degrees of pace and according to daily personal habits.

When a person who does mental work regularly has to be characterized, it is necessary to suggest physical

tension, which, in turn, produces certain body movement.   The arms will tend to hug the body and to be
folded, and the hands to be clasped in the pockets during
walking, with the shoulders hunched.   The arms will

Fig. 45

not swing freely and the scapula will be forward.   The
pace will be quick.   The character that does more
physical work than mental work will be more relaxed

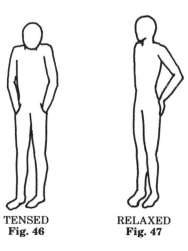

TENSED   RELAXED
Fig. 46   **Fig. 47**

physically, and, in turn, will reveal this with wider arm movement away from the body, with the elbows well out, the scapula back, and the head up. The pace will be slower.

Co-ordination of movement with opposition (Chapters III and VII) is apparent when the character is healthy and vital. Vitality wanes during fatigue and illness or with shock; then the arms dangle by the side

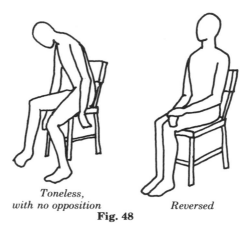

Toneless,
with no opposition   *Reversed*
Fig. 48

of the body, and walking or sitting movements are without opposition (Fig. 48). Emphasis of arms in opposition and well-pulled-back from the scapula, during movement, is involved in the characterization of a mannequin or any ultra-sophisticated person. The unsophisticated and the homely lack shoulder opposition and the arms tend to become straight with the body. The elbows, but not the scapula, are lifted: hence the elbows are turned outward during eating and drinking and the movements are quick. With the sophisticated and cultured, the elbows are in at the sides and

the movement is slow.   These mannerisms must not
be confused with the broad and constricted movements

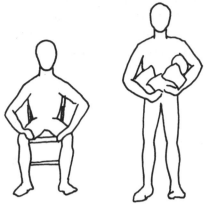

Unsophisticated — no shoulder opposition
Fig. 49

of the arms due to relaxation and tension mentioned
earlier in this chapter.

During walking the elbows similarly keep close to the

Sophisticated
Fig. 50

body. Opposition is apparent in their slight swing forward or backward. A handbag is not carried under the arm, but by the hand (Fig. 50). A homely character carries a parcel or a stout handbag under her arm, and, on sitting, either keeps them there or puts them on her lap. A sophisticated type places these on a chair, a table, or on the floor.

Old Age

The arms begin gradually to set or to become less flexible from the age of forty years. At first this loss in flexibility will be revealed by less movement from the

Fig. 51

scapula, and will not be noticed by the ageing person, but by the onlooker. As age advances, the loss increases, becomes apparent, and, ultimately, only restricted movement from the elbow is possible.

When a player sits the arms are bent and rigid at the elbow and remain so while he is seated. The arms are moved slightly and then only by necessity. The pace is extremely slow. There is no opposition of movement. The arms are square with the body. When a player rises from a chair, help is often given by the arms, supported by a stick or the seat or arms of the chair. When he stands, the arms, still bent and rigid at the elbow, come forward across the body. If there is movement from the scapula, it is slight; the scapula tending to be forward, so rounding the back (Fig. 51).

There is little or no swing, and no opposition during walking. Movement, if any, comes from the elbows only, which are kept to the body. If a stick is used, the movement is restricted, with a short distance between each point at which it is placed. With the scapula permanently forward, the shoulder girdle, coming forward and bringing the head with it, is rigid.

CHAPTER XVI

EYES AND MOUTH DURING YOUTH, MIDDLE AGE, AND OLD AGE

Youth

THE eyes are wide open and unblinking when the attention is held: they stare steadily at an object before moving to the next. The eyeballs move easily around the sockets, sometimes with a slight rolling upward movement. Frowning or raising the eyebrows rarely occurs. The brow is smooth and unlined. The

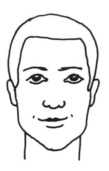

Fig. 52

mouth is relaxed and untensed, and the lips are full and slightly parted. There is no tension in the facial muscles, and the muscles round the mouth and chin are relaxed: during laughter the mouth opens and the head wobbles. When in repose, the mouth curves upward and dimples often appear (Fig. 52).

Middle Age

If the Emotional Scale is high—say 8–9—the eyes become fixed and staring, the forehead is lined, the eyebrows are drawn together or raised, and the facial muscles are rigid. The mouth is harmonized with the whole body, every muscle being at the same degree on the Emotional Scale. As tension increases, the mouth tightens and purses into a straight line. Small lines from the upper lip to the nose appear, also two strong lines from the outer edge of the mouth running

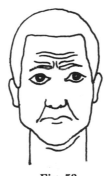

Fig. 53

to the outer side of each nostril. The corners of the mouth turn down, and two folds of flesh are noticeable on the lower sides of the chin. The lower half of the face has a downward slant (Fig. 53).

In contrast, contented eyes are relaxed and serene, the brow is smooth, untroubled; the mouth reposed and slightly parted, with the corners turning upward; the facial muscles are firm and tend to move upwards, just as at the beginning of a smile the whole face lifts. Much can be revealed by the set of the mouth. If tension is at 8 on the Emotional Scale, this must be revealed by the mouth, eyes, and facial muscles. With relaxation at, say, 3, the eyelids fall, and the mouth and facial muscles slacken completely.

Old Age

The corners of the eyes begin to show age by fine lines at the outer corners and "crow's feet" directly underneath the lower lid. As age increases, bags also

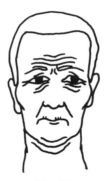

Fig. 54

appear, the forehead becomes lined, the lips lose their fullness and get thinner, and facial muscles droop. The whole face has a pulled-down look. A double chin is in evidence. The eyes, losing their brightness and sparkle, become dulled with little movement of the eyeballs. These tend to move more slowly and have a stationary look when focusing. Short sightedness causes the aged to peer. The range of movement is greatly restricted, the characteristic being immobility (Fig. 54).

CHAPTER XVII

THE HEAD DURING YOUTH, MIDDLE AGE, AND OLD AGE

THE way the head is carried and moved is important in expression. In youth the head turns, which are made with a wide and an easy rotary movement, are quick. For example, when a player looks round, the head is turned easily over the shoulder and is carried high. During middle age the turn is effected by a slower movement, and during old age there is little turn; the trunk, hips, shoulder, and head turn together in order to focus the eyes on their objective. The movement is slow. Tension will cause the head to lift or to droop. During high tension it will lift and on relaxation droop.

The Emotional Scale is the root mechanism by which the player is informed exactly how each member of the body reacts in given circumstances. A recurring tilt of the head to one side, a lifting or a lowering of the chin, and peering eyes all help to build a character. Most players have physical traits that repeat themselves in stage characterization according to temperament. These should be built up.

CHAPTER XVIII

WALKING DURING YOUTH, MIDDLE AGE, AND OLD AGE

CO-ORDINATION and freedom of movement when walking are indicative of a healthy mind and body that function harmoniously and without inhibition. Any part that is out of harmony (i.e. the mind, through anxiety, fatigue, sickness, shock, or the body, through pain or exhaustion) will be reflected by movements.

If tension is considerable, say 8–9 on the Emotional Scale, the movements will be staccato, inhibited, and quick; little opposition of movement will occur; co-ordination and economy of movement will disappear, and the walk will be stilted. If the feelings, such as those created by fatigue and sickness, lower the position on the Emotional Scale, co-ordination and the central balance of the body disappear. Two lines for placing the feet should be used (see Chapter I). No opposition occurs. The whole body tends to take the weight from side to side as the feet are placed, making a rolling, swaying movement. At, say, 3 on the Emotional Scale, the feet rarely come together on standing or sitting and regard for straight technique (see Chapter I) disappears.

In youth the walk is buoyant and springy. The head is carried high, the arms swing into opposition, the stride is long and from the hips, and the feet are placed on one line, with central balance (see Chapter I).

In middle age the tendency is to walk more from the knees and less from the hips, and two lines begin to be used for the feet, widening as age advances (see Chapter I). The feet start to turn outwards, there is less opposition of movement, the head has not the fine lift of youth, and the swing of the arms lessens. This general change is, at first, hardly perceptible, but a hint here and there is enough to indicate the age of the player, and

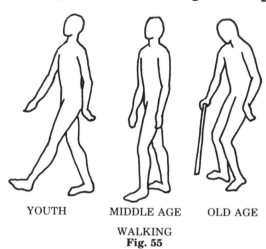

YOUTH   MIDDLE AGE   OLD AGE

WALKING
Fig. 55

change should be made more apparent as age increases.

The walk in old age becomes restricted. Movement is mainly from the knee joint. The joints are no longer braced back, but are bent and stiff. The balance of the whole body is thrown forward. The feet are flat, and are placed flatly, with the toes turned well out. The head is forward, the neck is short and pushed forward, the chest wall is narrow, and the shoulders are rounded. There is no opposition of movement, and one side of the body tends to be used more than the other : for example, the right foot, hip, shoulder, arm, hand, and ear

moving forward together to an objective.   The movements are extremely slow.   The act of putting on a
scarf, or a glove, or spectacles can be a performance in
itself.

Similar forward balance occurs during standing, with
feet well apart.   When the body has to be seated, it is
thrown forward and slowly lowered to the seat, the feet
and knees being well apart.   As men grow older, their
knees come together, but women's knees are kept wide
apart, this being particularly noticeable in a sitting
position.

CHAPTER XIX

THE BODY DURING YOUTH, MIDDLE AGE, AND OLD AGE

DURING the three phases, youth, middle age, and old age, the line of the body changes three times. In youth the line may be described as the S curve; in middle age it is straight; and in old age there is a curved line (Fig. 56).

Characteristics of the body in youth are suppleness and muscle tone, which enable the body to pull away from gravitation and to achieve the fine pose and uplift that are typical. The rotary movement is free, and no effort is required to turn from the waist whilst sitting in order to look behind. There is an absence of droop. Care should be taken by a player when portraying youth to accent the uplift and the fine tone of the whole body, as these are of its essence. Only when the Emotional Scale is under 5 does a slight droop occur.

A lifted chest wall, with scapulas drawn well back, a lifted diaphragm, and well-pulled-in abdominal muscles produce the S curve.

Imperceptibly, the body loses its fine pull away from gravitation during middle age. A slight "give", which occurs when the weight is transferred to each foot during walking, is noticeable first. Rotary trunk movements become less mobile, and the degree of turn is not so great. The scapulas are not so well braced, the chest wall drops slightly, the diaphragm begins to

collapse more often, and the abdominal muscles slacken.
The S curve begins to disappear and the straight line to
take its place.   Turning movements from the waist are
less frequent.   A player should bear in mind the degree
of these changes according to the age of the character to

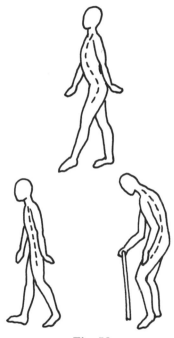

Fig. 56

be portrayed.   A hint makes a difference in portraying
a character of twenty-five, thirty-five, or forty-five
years of age.

In old age, the body has sagged through lack of
muscle tone, the scapulas are no longer braced back, the

chest wall has caved in, the diaphragm has collapsed, the abdominal muscles have slackened, and the curved line becomes permanent. Scarcely any rotary movements occur. Should the character have to turn to the the right or to the left, the turn is made by stepping with the feet in the direction of the object, the body remaining immobile and almost rigid.

CHAPTER XX

DRAMATIC PAUSE WITH EMOTIONAL SCALE

DRAMATIC pause is caused by the sudden occurrence of news that brings a reaction which either tenses or relaxes. If the hopes of the character are high and are suddenly dashed, the impact of the opposite feeling causes a pause while the mind, descending the Emotional Scale, takes in the impact slowly until it becomes a realized fact. Not until *this* occurs is the dramatic pause broken by movement or speech. First the mind changes its attitude; then, on realization, speech and movement occur on precisely the degree of the Scale to which the thoughts have risen or fallen.

Suppose a character is waiting for news of a loved one who is seriously ill. He hopes against hope that the news will be good. He is at 9 on the Scale. The news is given: "She is dead." Hope stops. He cannot at first take in the news, which he accepts gradually. Hope is dead, too; his emotions come down the scale 9, 8, 7, 6, 5, 4, 3, 2, 1, and he faints.

Consider the opposite experience.

He waits to hear the news of the death of his beloved for whom there is no hope. Completely hopeless, he is at 3 on the Scale. The news arrives: "She will recover." His mind begins to take it in, hope returns, thoughts regather, his spirits rise, 3, 4, 5, 6, 7, 8, 9. That she will live becomes a fact registered at 10.   He moves and speaks simultaneously: "She will live!"

Again, the voice must be controlled so that it is not taken over 10; otherwise a squeak will result.

Here is an exercise that is designed to help timing and speech during the dramatic pause. A, with high tension, is on the stage alone.   B, low on the Emotional Scale, enters and gives the news.   Pause, during which A descends the Scale, and then speaks on movement.

Reverse the scene and repeat, with A on the stage at 2, and B entering at 9 giving the news, which, during the pause, will take A to 10, after which he will show with movement and speech exactly what has happened to him during the pause.   Fear must not be felt at the seeming length of the pause, fear, say, of losing the audience's attention, for it is at this very moment, when the player's attention is caught and held, that he holds his audience most powerfully.   Robert Helpmann, who so superbly controls and recognizes the power of the dramatic pause and knows the full value of economy of movement, should be watched for these points.

CHAPTER XXI

CO-ORDINATION OF SPEECH WITH MOVEMENT

THE perfect timing of speech with movement is both delightful and important. Movement ceases with the end of a sentence. A player should neither speak and then move nor move and then speak. He must move and speak *simultaneously*, and both speech and movement must cease together. Perfect timing does not permit of one fraction of difference between the two endings. For example, on the question "Why?" the head turns on the word, not after or before, but *as* it is spoken.

"I simply must sit down." Here a player feels the chair with the back of his knee on "simply", closes his feet on "must", sits at the word "sit", makes his final knee crossing and leans back on "down", and then is still. The sentence is timed and phrased with the movement.

Suppose a player has to cross a wide stage on the short sentence, "Charles, do you love me?" The move is from down stage L to down stage R in front of the firegrate. If she asked the question at once as she began to move, the second half of the stage would be crossed in silence and attention would be divided or lost. She should start to move on "Charles," pause on speech, continue to move to the fireplace, and on reaching it, turn to Charles and ask "Do you love me?", ending her turn absolutely dead on "me".

Here is a helpful exercise.

Sit on a chair and talk to another player, each player co-ordinating movement and speech: the dialogue indicates the kind of move, whether high or low on the Emotional Scale. One player says: "I am tired." "Tired" is the key-word. He leans back and relaxes to 3. "How wonderful," she exclaims, this bringing her forward and upright to 7, and so on. The dialogue must be combed through. These mechanics can be applied on making an entrance.

The player, sure of the exact mood for his entrance, should begin to create it in his dressing-room, develop it, remain in it as he walks to the wings to await his cue, and then enter. If the entrance is made at, say, 4, the voice and movement reveal the mood, which should not depend solely on the meaning in the lines. If the player tries to get into his mood *as* he opens the door to make his entrance, he will fail.

When his entry is made on dialogue, it should be phrased with his movement during the mechanics of the opening and shutting of the door (see Chapter VIII). He should be concentrated on the mood and the objective, and not on the manipulation of the door. If it is not, the entrance will be ineffective.

Similar principles apply to the making of an exit. The door must be approached during dialogue; otherwise the player will cross and exit in silence. Interest must be sustained. For example, if the last line before the exit is "*Au revoir*—to-night at 8.30", the player should begin to cross to the exit on "*Au revoir*", pause his speech until he opens the door, and time speech and movement on "To-night at 8.30", as the door closes.

CHAPTER XXII

STAGE EMBRACES

WHEN a man takes a woman into his arms during
a standing embrace, his weight is forward and her
weight is backward. This enables the woman's head
and shoulders to fall back and her hips to come forward.
If this is reversed and her weight is forward, her head

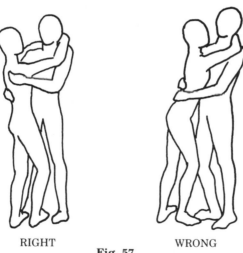

RIGHT   WRONG

Fig. 57

and shoulders come forward and her hips are pushed
back, giving a grotesque and ugly line (Fig. 57).

The mechanics of the exercise are simple. The man
stands with his feet well apart, with the R foot a little

SITTING EMBRACE: RIGHT
Fig. 58

SITTING EMBRACE: WRONG
Fig. 59

forward, and his weight upon it, and with the L shoulder and hip forward.

The woman steps between the man's feet with her R foot and L shoulder and hip forward, simultaneously drawing her L foot behind her R foot in order to maintain her balance as the man leans forward and embraces her, taking her shoulders and head back as he does so.

The man's L arm encircles the woman's waist and her L arm the man's neck. The right hand may lie on his L elbow or coat lapel, but should be kept lower than her L arm.

The hips of each player should touch. The farther the woman takes the step between the man's feet, the easier it is to control the balance.

Next exercise with the L foot first and apply similar mechanics of movement but in reverse. If the woman relaxes as she steps forward, the man is able to pivot and to swing her as desired.

CHAPTER XXIII

CLIMAX

BUILDING a climax is a scientific plan mechanically carried out. The architecture is built up slowly but surely. The responsibility of each player is to understand the cause and effect of each detail and its contribution to the whole. It is not enough for the player to give a moving interpretation *his* way, if it is not in harmony with the whole. The perfect teamwork of give and take makes the perfect whole. The producer should give the players his plan. Then they should relate the script to the Emotional Scale. Mounting should be steady, all keeping more or less to the same tension, 4, 6, or 8, and arriving at 10, the climax *par excellence*, TOGETHER. For example, if there are six players on the stage before the climax and one continues to play at 4, he will not only divide attention but also ultimately hold it as the "odd man out". Similarly, if the scene is at a tension of 4 and one player remains at 9, it fails. The mechanics of the 1–10 Emotional Scale help to make realization of the climax comparatively simple. Feelings are misleading. Build without them. When sure of the structure, add the feelings; be aware of them and forget the structure. When a player is sure of himself, he can afford to forget the mechanics— and can *feel*. In other words, through discipline freedom is realized.

The Bow

When the bow is taken at the end of a performance, the players should be standing down stage centre behind the line of the curtain, with the feet together, the arms at the side, and the knees braced. The bow comes from the waist. The head, neck, shoulders, and arms relax as the body comes forward, but the knees remain braced. Lower the trunk slowly, counting up to four. Raise slowly with the same *tempo* of four counts, simultaneously straightening the spine, taking back the shoulders and the neck, and, lastly, lifting the head. The bow may be repeated, turning the trunk to the R, repeated again to the L, and finally, to the gallery with the head well lifted, this time to catch the eyes of the gallery audience, and to give a smile.

For a further curtain call for the entire cast, there should be a rehearsal, under direction of the producer, of the places to be taken by the characters. A small semicircle should be formed, or a straight line, if the cast is small. The centre player should give the cue for the bow. The same *tempo* should be maintained by all with the same depth of bow; four counts down and four up will help to maintain unity. The technique of movement as described at the beginning of the chapter should be used. A curtain call in which each player takes the bow at his own pace and depth is untidy and unfinished.

Unity of pace and movement will result in a dignified and finished curtain call.

CURTAIN

INDEX TO ACTING

INDEX TO STAGE MOVEMENT

180